THE ABCs
OF WORSHIP

THE ABCs
OF WORSHIP

A CONCISE DICTIONARY

DONALD WILSON STAKE

WESTMINSTER/JOHN KNOX PRESS
LOUISVILLE, KENTUCKY

BOOK DESIGN BY
Kristen Dietrich

FIRST EDITION

Published by Westminster/John Knox Press
Louisville, Kentucky

This book is printed on acid-free paper that meets the American National Standards Institute Z39.48 standard. ∞

PRINTED IN THE UNITED STATES OF AMERICA
2 4 6 8 9 7 5 3 1

Library of Congress Cataloging-in-Publication Data

Stake, Donald Wilson, 1935–
  The ABCs of worship : a concise dictionary / Donald Wilson Stake.
—1st ed.
     p.   cm.
  Includes bibliographical references.
  ISBN 0-664-25246-X

  1. Public worship—Dictionaries. I. Title.
BV15.S69 1992
264′ .003—dc20
91-45294

FOR

MARY JANE

INTRODUCTION

The people of the church I serve have raised many questions about worship. They want to know why changes are made and sometimes why they are not made. Mostly they want to know why we worship the way we do and why Christians down the street do it differently.

All these questions have provoked my liturgical education, which shows every sign of needing to continue. Again and again, I have sought out resources and friends to give me some answers for my curious people. I have come to realize that people are not merely curious. They have an investment in worship. It belongs to them, and anyone—pastor or governing board—responsible for their worship had better have answers. That is as it should be.

I have also discovered that my own curiosity about worship is similarly healthy. Knowing some of the "whys" makes my leadership more effective and enhances my worship as well.

What is at issue is the renewal of worship. Indeed, the issue is the renewal of the church. The people in the pews take worship seriously. So do pastors. Worship defines who we are as the church of Jesus Christ in this world and is not to be taken lightly.

The Reformation continues. No longer, however, is it simply a Protestant process. Roman Catholic and Orthodox Christians join with Protestants of all shades and shapes, including Pentecostals, charismatics, evangelicals, and many others, in rediscovering the centrality of worship to the Christian faith. The modern ecumenical movement allows us to learn from each other. In fact, we can no longer wear

1

blinders and forget the others with whom we share the name "Christian." We are mutually enriched by shared and differing traditions. The Holy Spirit draws us together and surprises us with fresh visions and insights from our neighbors. Our liturgical renewal is an exciting gift from God.

This book is intended to contribute to the process of renewal in a small but significant way. It was written because people asked, "Why?" It attempts to give some basic answers in clear, nontechnical language so that worshipers will have a better sense of what they are doing.

Readers of this book should be challenged to turn to other more comprehensive and more competent resources. Pastors, lay leaders, musicians, and people in the pews will find an appetizer of information here preliminary to a banquet that awaits. The reference list "For Further Reading" points to the feast. This book offers an introduction only. There is much more to learn.

The book is arranged in dictionary form for convenience. Cross-references tie the entries together like a web. Start anywhere and you can follow the strands throughout most if not all aspects of worship. Worship has an integrity, a unity, that is plain to see in the connections the cross-references make.

This book is written from the perspective of the Reformed tradition. Part of what we understand it to mean to be Reformed is that we need to be informed. The Reformed tradition also reflects a certain theological slant tilted in the direction of John Calvin. At the same time, Reformed means "reforming" and therefore open to the working of the Holy Spirit. Readers will find other perspectives here as well and an ecumenical openness that welcomes enlightenment from whatever source.

I thank God for opportunities to worship, especially those I regularly experience with the people of Union Presbyterian Church in Schenectady. I am gratified by their challenging questions, which keep me asking my own as I worship and study with them. I also thank God for the people of three other congregations. St. John the Baptist Roman Catholic Church in Schenectady is bound to Union Presbyterian

Church in a formal covenant, in which we are committed to worship together at various times. Pastor Robert LeFevre is a trusted colleague and good friend. Congregation Agudat Achim of Schenectady graciously hosts our congregation on many occasions and just as graciously accepts our hospitality as we worship God together. Rabbi Samuel Kieffer is a scholar to envy and a friend to cherish. The Monastery of New Skete in Cambridge, New York, provides me an experience of rich liturgy in the Eastern Orthodox tradition and a warm welcome on occasions that are, for me, too infrequent. Father Laurence and the monks, nuns, and lay members of the community are generous with their faith and friendship.

I am indebted to Harold Daniels, of the Theology and Worship Unit of the Presbyterian Church (U.S.A.), who was kind enough to review this manuscript in its various incarnations. He has generously shared information, wisdom, encouragement, and especially friendship.

Most of all, I thank God for my wife Mary Jane, who had the idea for this book in the first place and who asks the questions that keep me humble.

May God's grace continue to renew our faith, that our worship in the name of Jesus Christ may truly be service, by the power of the Holy Spirit.

D.W.S.

Ascension Day 1991

Acclamation.

An acclamation is a liturgical form of applause—not literally clapping hands but the congregation's using words to praise God. During the Great Prayer of Thanksgiving at the Lord's Supper, specifically, the congregation interjects its acclaim of Christ:

> Christ has died,
> Christ is risen,
> Christ will come again.

Another version is known as the Memorial Acclamation:

> Dying, You destroyed our death;
> Rising, You restored our life.
> Lord Jesus, come in glory.

The acclamation serves as a lens to bring the faith into sharp focus at the heart of Christian worship. By use of the acclamation, the congregation at the Lord's Supper remembers the redemptive death of Christ, celebrates the presence of the risen Christ, and anticipates the return of Christ to rule. (*See also* Great Prayer of Thanksgiving; Lord's Supper.)

Advent.

The season of Advent begins the Christian Year. The four Sundays preceding Christmas mark a time of preparation. *Advent* comes from a Latin word meaning "coming" or "arrival." The color is purple, signifying royalty as Christians gather to get ready for the coming of Christ, who is to reign over all the universe. Sometimes the color blue, symbolic of hope, is used.

The main preparation Christians make to welcome Christ anew into their lives is through self-examination and repentance. Advent is a season of penitence (another reason for the use of the color purple). It is similar in purpose to Lent and was modeled on it. Christians remember their own need for God to come again in their lives, confessing their sin and separation from God, and expressing deep longing for what God alone can give, the gift of new life and salvation.

Advent is a time to remember that we also wait for Christ to come again. We are still sinners in need of redemption. The whole world longs for peace and justice. We continue to look for Jesus Christ to come save us.

Part of Advent is the celebration of John the Baptist's ministry as the one who came to announce Christ and to call people to repentance. John the Baptist personifies Advent.

The Advent wreath is a visual symbol of waiting for the coming of Christ. As we draw nearer to Christmas, spiritual light increases and the darkness is chased away, symbolized by the lighting of the candles, one the first week, two the second, and so forth. Usually the candles are purple although other colors are sometimes used. The third candle may be pink, a color associated with joy. This reminds us of one of the texts appointed since the Middle Ages for this day, Philippians 4:4–6, which begins with the word "rejoice." In the midst of the season of penitence, the pink candle reminds us that there is yet cause for rejoicing in the impending coming of God in Jesus Christ. (*See also* Christian Year; Christmas; O Antiphons.)

Affirmation of Faith.

At the time of a baptism, the faith of the church is affirmed by the one being baptized, or by parents or sponsors for that person. In Western churches this affirmation usually takes the form of the Apostles' Creed, while in the Eastern churches the Nicene Creed is customarily used. Such affirmation follows the Renunciation of Evil. Turning away from evil, one turns toward Christ. (*See also* Baptism; Confession of Faith; Creed; Renunciation of Evil.)

Agape Meal.

Agape is a Greek word meaning "love," specifically, divine love. An agape meal is a time of fellowship among God's people when they celebrate God's love for them, which in turn enables them to love one another.

The agape meal began early in the church's life as followers of the risen Christ continued to gather for common meals. When they did, they remembered Christ, and in giving thanks and breaking bread to share, they remembered the countless times he was host at the table with them.

They also remembered the Last Supper and the commandment of Jesus to "do this in remembrance" of him. They broke bread and shared a cup of wine in what came to be known as the Lord's Supper. Apparently in the beginning the agape meal and the Lord's Supper took place together (see 1 Corinthians 11).

The time came, however, when the church separated the two. The agape meal continued to be a time of fellowship for the people of the church. The Lord's Supper was specifically a remembering of Jesus Christ's death and resurrection, and it became more ritualized and connected to the prayers and scripture of the weekly worship of the community. This observance took place on Sunday, the Lord's Day, the day of resurrection.

The agape meal persisted, its modern descendant being the church supper. This pot-luck sharing signals the agape meal theme of God's love shared with us. Often such fellowship meals begin with a brief ritual that points to God's love. Luke 9:12–17 is an appropriate passage to be read, followed by a brief prayer of thanks to God for the Bread of Life, Jesus Christ. This prayer might begin with a version of the traditional Jewish prayer at a meal, such as: "Blessed are you, O Lord our God, Ruler of the universe, for you cause the earth to yield food for all." Bread may be broken and shared among the people before the people are served the meal. At the end of the meal, another prayer is offered concluding with the Lord's Prayer and dismissal. (*See also* Blessing; Koinonia; Lord's Day/Sunday/Sabbath; Lord's Supper.)

Agnus Dei.

Agnus Dei is Latin for "Lamb of God," referring to Christ as the lamb sacrificed in our place to atone or pay for our sins. The text is a part of Christian liturgy dating from the seventh century, based on the announcement of John the Baptist about Jesus in John 1:29:

> Lamb of God, you take away the sin of the world,
>   have mercy upon us.
> Lamb of God, you take away the sin of the world,
>   have mercy upon us.
> Lamb of God, you take away the sin of the world,
>   grant us peace.

This is appropriately sung as a piece of service music by the choir and/or congregation during communion as a way of remembering Christ's sacrifice. It may also be sung as a hymn. (*See also* Lord's Supper.)

Alb.

See Vestments/Robes/Stoles.

All Saints Day.

November 1 is All Saints Day, when the church celebrates the witness of those people of God who have gone before us in faith. It has its origin in feasts observed as early as the fifth century. At first the feast honoring martyrs was connected with Easter and Pentecost, but the November date was established in the West about the ninth century; in the Eastern Orthodox tradition it is still observed the week after Pentecost. While the day originally emphasized commemoration of those who were martyred for their witness to Christ (*martyr* is the Greek word meaning "witness"), it is to include glad remembrance of all God's faithful people who have died.

This is a day to remember that we are one in the "communion of saints" with the church through all ages. Rejoicing in God's presence with the faithful in the past, we happily affirm God's powerful presence with us now. We are encouraged by the persistence and fidelity of those who have gone before us. They urge us on in our ministry as a "cloud of witnesses" (Hebrews 12:1). It is appropriate on this day to give thanks for the lives of those among us who have died in the past year.

The color is white, indicating faithfulness and suggesting that the risen Christ who lives in and through the saints is the One we praise. This is very different from veneration of the saints in the medieval Roman Catholic sense, which suggests that they are mediators to be enlisted on our behalf before God. Most Protestants do not pray *to* the saints but give thanks *for* them. They are a continuing sign of God's grace and the power of the Holy Spirit sustaining the church.

The marching hymn for this day is "For All the Saints."

All Souls' Day in Protestant practice has been absorbed into All Saints' Day. It was originally a separate feast, established in the Middle Ages and observed on November 2, to honor those dead who were not martyred or distinguished by some special witness. They were believed to be in purgatory, unlike the saints who were in heaven. In Protestant thought no such distinction is made; all who have died in the Lord are considered saints. (*See also* Saints.)

Altar.

The altar is different from the Table on which the Lord's Supper is celebrated, yet the difference is perhaps more in emphasis than in substance. An altar is, by definition, a place where a sacrifice is offered. In Reformed worship the Table is central, and the Lord's Supper does commemorate the sacrifice of Christ on behalf of humankind, so in this sense the

Table may be thought of as an altar. Yet the Reformers rejected the notion that the priest re-offered the sacrifice of Christ on the altar at each Mass. The Table was rather understood as the place to gather for a meal in obedience to Christ's command to break bread and share wine in "remembering" what Christ has done once and for all. The sacrifice is God's act, not ours. Table is a safer designation than altar for it prevents us from presuming that we can recreate God's sacrifice of love. We only celebrate it; we do not make it happen.

In the early centuries of Christianity, many followers of Jesus Christ paid for their faith with their lives. Witnessing to Jesus Christ was sometimes tantamount to being killed, so vicious was the persecution. The term *martyr* meant "witness" and was applied to those who died for their faith. Some of the early martyrs were buried in the catacombs where other Christians, fleeing persecution, worshiped. The stone tombs were sometimes used as the Tables for celebrating the Lord's Supper. The sacrifice of the martyrs was painfully obvious to the worshipers. Still, it was clear that their sacrifice was only in response to the ultimate and self-sufficient sacrifice of Jesus Christ on the cross. What God did there made their own faithful martyrdoms possible.

Church architecture and the arrangement and designation of furniture communicate theology. A communion table pushed against the wall may appear to be an altar. If the monetary offering is placed on this altar-table, then the sacrifices of the people may eclipse the sacrifice of God's Son. (*See also* Lord's Supper; Offering.)

Amen.

The word *amen* is a Hebrew word used in the Old Testament (see 1 Chron. 16:35–36; 1 Kings 1:36; Neh. 8:6; and Ps. 106:48, for example) and found in Greek in the New Testament as well (see 1 Cor. 14:16).

In the Jewish tradition, "Amen" in Hebrew is considered by some to be an acronym for "God, our faithful King" and can be used as a confession of one's faith. Similarly, Christians might remember that "Amen" is a name applied to Christ (Rev. 3:14), who is our faithful King. In saying "Amen," we affirm our faith in him.

Amen is also a prayer and may be translated "let it be so" (see Rev. 22:20). At the end of a statement of faith, for example, the people's "Amen" is a prayer that what they have affirmed will come true.

In some Christian churches "Amen!" is used with enthusiasm. The people respond to a prayer or a sermon, adding their personal "amens" to the words spoken by another. It is an affirmation, an assent, even a subscription as though they were signing their names. "Amen" always implies a commitment as well, for acceptance leads one to action.

"Amen" is sometimes used at the end of hymns although that use is a recent custom dating back only to the nineteenth century. In many newer hymnals the "Amen" has been dropped. "Amen" at the end of a hymn tends to be used as vocal punctuation, sung without zeal. An upbeat, affirmative hymn can be undercut by a tired "Amen." Besides, the word is redundant since the people themselves have already sung the hymn and there is no need for them to reaffirm it with their "Amen."

The people's "Amen" at the end of a prayer spoken by another is an ancient act of worship worthy of our use today. For in this way we affirm the corporate nature of our worship. When the people say "Amen" to a prayer that one person articulates, it becomes clear that it is not one person praying instead of the rest but one person leading the prayers of all. (*See also* Confession of Faith; Cross, Sign of; Hymn; Prayer.)

Anamnesis (Remembrance).

Anamnesis is a Greek word meaning "remembrance." Paul quotes Jesus as giving the bread and wine at the Last Supper with the instructions to eat and drink in "remembrance" (*anamnesis*) of him (1 Cor. 11:24–25). Specifically, the term refers to that essential part of the Great Prayer of

Thanksgiving remembering the redemptive sacrifice of Jesus Christ.

The word *anamnesis* is really untranslatable because it means much more than simply remembering. It suggests that by eating the bread and drinking the wine as instructed by Jesus, the past becomes present. The Lord's Supper is not a memorial in the sense that we think about what happened long ago but is a recalling of the death and resurrection of Christ to be experienced in the present. We do not simply honor One who died nearly twenty centuries ago but encounter One who is risen and present with us even now. *Anamnesis* is our experience of Christ present in the Lord's Supper. Because it has this particular meaning, the word *anamnesis* is used rather than any English word that can at best be only an approximation. (*See also* Great Prayer of Thanksgiving; Lord's Supper.)

Announcements.

What do we do with announcements in the worship service? One answer is "nothing" since announcements would seem to have nothing to do with worship. Another answer is to place all announcements before the beginning of the service so as not to intrude upon the flow of the service. This may seem distracting, however, in that it may shift attention to housekeeping matters from the purpose for which the community is gathered, namely worship. Yet another practice is to make announcements at the conclusion of the service, as a transition from the life of the congregation gathered for worship to the life of the congregation dispersed for witness and service.

Another answer that has integrity is to place the announcements immediately before the prayers of intercession, sometimes called "the prayers of the people." The announcements become a way of offering up to God the life of the congregation and of the whole church as an act of worship.

Included in announcements might be:

The welcome of visitors to the congregation. As the act of worship establishes the people gathered as the church, the

Body of Christ, so the welcome of visitors is the extending of God's hospitality to strangers and the reminder that the church catholic includes all Christians from whatever congregation.

The announcement of needs of people in the congregation. When there are illnesses or deaths or other special needs, these may be announced as the prelude to prayers offered on behalf of the people involved.

The announcement of needs in the world and community. The world around us is always in need, and the church is called to be responsive to that need in the name of Christ. In this way the need is brought before God, to pray for those in need, and thereby offer commitment to work in practical ways to meet that need.

The announcement of activities or events in the life of the congregation. As the people gather they become the Body of Christ, the church. This community has a life of fellowship, nurture, and mission, and all its life is appropriately offered to God in the context of worship, for it is from the worship of the people gathered that the congregation receives its life in the Spirit.

(*See also* Bulletin; Intercession, Prayers of.)

Anointing.

Anointing is the placing of oil on a person's head. Roman Catholic, Episcopal, and many modern Protestant liturgies for baptism provide for this action as a symbol that the one baptized belongs to Christ (Christ literally means "Anointed One"). The sick are anointed to remind them of the fact of their baptism and that they belong to Christ. This is obedient to the injunction in James 5:14.

The Reformers did not take kindly to anointing as a part of the baptismal service. They felt it was distracting and that it had acquired an almost sacramental status of its own. Today, however, the act of anointing is understood as a symbol used to emphasize what has happened in baptism and is in no way to be considered its equivalent. Anointing can be effective in communicating to all present the message that in baptism we all belong to Christ, the Anointed One of God. (*See also* Baptism; Cross, Sign of; Oil; Service for Wholeness.)

Anthem.

The anthem is a song of praise sung by the choir, as distinguished from hymns and other songs sung by the congregation. It is important that the anthem be sung by the choir not as a performance for the congregation but on behalf of the congregation as worship of God. Traditionally anthems are based on scriptural texts or at the very least elaborate on the theme of praise. The emphasis should be on the anthem's purpose of divine praise. Choral selections that focus narrowly on the seasons or phenomena of nature or human emotion are inadequate to the praise of God in Christian worship.

Sometimes choirs aim too low. They think they are performing for the benefit of the congregation. When choirs remember that their purpose is to please God with their singing and not to entertain the people, then their singing is lifted to a higher plane. God is the true audience of all we do in worship, including our singing. So the choir—made up of the better voices of the congregation and people ready to commit themselves to rehearsal in advance—represents and leads the congregation in its musical offerings to God.

Anthems today usually appear at two places in the order of service: an anthem of praise at the beginning of the service or an anthem of praise and dedication at the time of the offering. While essentially all anthems are songs of praise, they may emphasize various aspects of worship such as confession of sin, confession of faith, thanksgiving, and proclamation. (*See also* Choir; Music; Musician; Service for the Lord's Day.)

Antiphon.

Originally a Greek word meaning "responsive," an antiphon is thought of today as one of two things. It may refer to a kind of singing (or speaking) back and forth between two groups alternating parts. More commonly, an antiphon is a refrain sung with a psalm. Antiphons enable a variety of expression and a presentation of sung scriptural texts in dialogue form. Antiphonal singing helps involve the whole congregation in the liturgy. (*See also* Musician; O Antiphons; Psalms.)

Apostles' Creed.

See Confession of Faith; Creed.

Apse.

The *apse* of a church is that part of the worship space that is on the other side of the table from the congregation. It is technically an architectural term referring to a semicircular extension of the room capped by a half dome.

The apse provides a defined space for the one who presides (in ancient times, the bishop) to stand behind the table facing the people. This arrangement is in contrast to placing the table against a flat back wall as an altar. In this case the presiding minister, when facing the altar, would of necessity face away from the people. The apse, common in Syrian and Roman churches, became a common feature in churches of the Middle Ages. (*See also* Altar; Table.)

Art.

While the subject of art may be broadly conceived to include a variety of modes of expression, this discussion of art in worship will be restricted to visual art. Drama, dance, and music are art as well in the broadest sense of the word but are treated separately.

The Protestant Reformers were not kindly disposed to what we would call visual art. Rather than seeing it as an aid to worship, they saw it as a distraction at best and a hindrance at worst. There came a time when many Protestants literally cleared churches of all representations of any kind: they smashed sculptures, covered murals, and removed anything remotely ornate. Protestant churches became austere and even bare.

As a reaction to an abuse, this radical action had much to commend it, but it became an overreaction in many ways. The Reformers did away with visual representations because they were often misused in the medieval church. People invested images with magical powers, statues became objects of prayers, and the whole worship space was often cluttered and confusing. The crucifix (a cross with a realistic figure of the crucified Christ on it) was commonly used in Western churches by the fifteenth century. Stations of the Cross developed during and after the crusades as tableaux of the last journey of Christ to the cross, erected in churches to inspire the devotions of the faithful. Both reflected a subjective piety immersed in the suffering of Christ. The Reformers, however, emphasized the objective triumph of Christ on the cross. While Lutherans kept crosses for ceremonial and even ornamental purposes, Calvinists generally rejected their use until the twentieth century. In doing away with visual imagery in the churches, the Reformers affirmed that art is not to be a substitute for righteousness and that the people themselves are sufficient representation of the image of God. The only other visual signs needed are the elements of the sacraments.

This is all well taken even today. Nevertheless, we have learned that art can be an aid to worship if properly used. The artist engages in a personal act of worship by creating a particular work, which in turn inspires others. Visual representations in sculpture, design, or symbol may inform and edify the worshiper, enhancing the meaning of a biblical text or a seasonal theme.

Anyone who has seen stained glass windows in great churches and cathedrals can appreciate this. Stained glass windows may be thought of as an architectural form of filmstrip in which the separate frames are combined to tell a biblical story. Orthodox Christians use paintings called icons to represent people of faith of previous generations and to tell stories from scripture. These become teaching tools as children come to worship with the full community.

Banners are popular these days because they are relatively inexpensive to construct and they bring vivid colors to brighten worship space. Furthermore, unlike windows, they may be changed according to season or emphasis. They should be considered as art and fashioned from quality materials.

Sculpture and framed paintings are less frequently seen in Protestant places of worship. A portable statue that can be displayed well or a painting of such size to be seen throughout the congregation might be useful as a thematic statement or as the focus for a point in a sermon.

More subtle yet in some ways the most significant is the overall decor of the worship space. Lighting, whether exterior or artificial, is of critical importance. Colors used in furniture, wall coverings, stained glass windows, pew cushions, and carpets must be selected with great care so as to work with seasonal colors and decorations. Choir and clergy robes and vestments must also take into account the context of the room's decor. The way the room looks without seasonal or special decoration will create a basic mood or atmosphere that will influence and affect all other uses of art.

It is helpful for a church to give an arts committee the responsibility to oversee the acquisition or production of visual art for worship and for use throughout the church building. The committee may establish criteria for art in the church. Local artists and teachers can be of considerable assistance in this. The committee will want to develop a list of people in the congregation who have artistic skills and encourage them to create specific works as they are needed. Funding may well be provided by memorial or other special contributions. It is better to purchase or create original art than it is to buy from catalogs, so that the art will be appropriate for the particular worship space. (*See also* Bulletin; Colors; Decorations; Symbols; Vestments/Robes/Stoles.)

Ascension Day.

Within the season of Easter we celebrate Ascension Day, forty days after Easter Day (see Acts 1:3–11). The One who was crucified and raised again to new life is now lifted to glory and power, and Christ's followers are promised the gift of Holy Spirit. This day proclaims the fullness of Easter, for Jesus Christ is risen to rule over all creation, seated at the right hand of God Almighty.

Ascension Day is always on a Thursday but may be remembered in Lord's Day worship the Sunday before Pentecost, when the scripture lessons for Ascension Day may be used. Ascension Day thereby helps us to anticipate Pentecost. (*See also* Christian Year; Easter.)

Ash Wednesday.

Ash Wednesday marks the beginning of the season of Lent, forty days (not counting Sundays) before Easter. Its name comes from the practice of placing ashes on Christians as a sign of their penitence. The practice was common to the ancient Hebrews (see Jonah 3:6, for example) as well as in New Testament times (see Matt. 11:21). Christian use of ashes as a symbol of penitence goes back at least to the second century. By the fifth century Ash Wednesday was established.

While the period of Lent began as a time of preparation for those planning to profess their faith at Easter, Ash Wednesday was for the whole community. It is in itself a time of preparation for Lent. The ashes remind us of our own mortality. As they are applied to the forehead of the Christian, it is customary to recite "Remember that you are dust and to dust you shall return" (see Gen. 3:19). This sets the believer on a sobering time of self-examination and repentance, to wait upon the renewal given by God's Spirit in the death and resurrection of Jesus Christ.

Ashes are traditionally made by burning the palm branches from the previous Palm Sunday. The color for Ash Wednesday is usually purple as for the rest of Lent, but sometimes gray, the color of ashes, is used.

The day before Ash Wednesday is sometimes called "Shrove Tuesday." *Shrove* comes from an Anglo-Saxon word referring to confession and the imposition of penance. This day is observed in some traditions as a time of confession in anticipation of the season of Lent.

Another name for the day before Ash Wednesday is "Fat Tuesday" ("Mardi Gras"). This refers to the practice of using up all foods that cannot be eaten during the Lenten fast. In Protestant circles this is symbolized by the pancake suppers often held on that day. A parallel symbol is found in the pancake breakfasts on Easter Sunday morning, which signify breaking the fast of Lent. (*See also* Cross, Sign of; Lent.)

Assurance of Pardon.

See Declaration of Forgiveness.

Baptism.

One of the two sacraments recognized by most Christians, baptism is the rite of initiation by which a person becomes a part of the Body of Christ, the church. In the early centuries of the church, baptisms were celebrated at the Easter Vigil after a period of preparation that ultimately became Lent.

Baptism is a sacrament because it was mandated by Jesus Christ himself (Matt. 28:18–20). We baptize, not as a way of coercing God's grace but in response to the grace of God who calls us to be people of God. Baptism, therefore, is not at our initiative but God's. God claims us for Christian discipleship. In baptism we acknowledge and celebrate that claim.

Baptism is an expression of the intimate relationship between God and the people of God. The person baptized is welcomed into the fellowship of faith, and the congregation, on behalf of the whole church, accepts responsibility for the Christian nurture of the baptized person. For this reason baptism is to be celebrated in corporate worship and not privately.

In baptism we are made part of the whole people of God. Baptism is the sign and seal of our covenant with God and God's covenant with us. It is the Christian equivalent of circumcision but is inclusive of females.

When an infant is baptized, the divine initiative is stressed. When an adult is baptized, it is still clear that what is signified is not the individual's volunteering for service as much as a divine conscription and the person's reporting for duty. Parents, guardians, and sponsors of an infant to be baptized witness to their own faith that God calls the child to be part of the family of the church, to be nurtured in faith and trained in discipleship. Adults baptized also need the continuing encouragement of the community as they grow in faith.

The congregation plays an important role in baptism, for promises are made by the members of the particular church for the whole church—promises to care for and nurture the baptized person (child or adult) in the faith. This is why, in Reformed churches, baptisms are always in the presence of the congregation at worship. The Christian education program of any church is a major part of the fulfillment of this promise.

Counseling by the pastor and/or church leaders precedes baptism. Candidates for baptism, or their parents and sponsors, make vows, not only to follow Jesus Christ, as they affirm the faith of the church, but also to turn away from all that is wrong in the world, as they renounce evil. All confess their faith using the traditional Apostles' Creed, which originated as a baptismal creed (Eastern churches traditionally use the Nicene Creed).

In the service of baptism, water is used generously. Baptism is a bath. It is washing with water. A sufficient amount of water should be used so this significance can be recognized by all present. In baptism we are washed clean of sin and given a new and unsullied life.

In many Protestant churches, "sprinkling" (pouring water out of the cupped hand) is the usual mode although "pouring" directly from a pitcher or large cruet over the person's head into the font and total "immersion" are also appropriate. Baptism by immersion, practiced by Baptists, Orthodox, and other Christians, demonstrates the meaning of dying, being buried (under water), and being raised again to new life in Christ (see Rom. 6:3–4.) When baptism by immersion is de-

sired in a congregation where this is not the common practice, it may be necessary to borrow the worship space of a
nearby church with appropriate facilities. A nearby stream or
river might also be used if arrangements are made to ensure a
worshipful atmosphere. Such an event should be set for
morning worship on the Lord's Day, even if it must be at a
time different from the usual worship hour. It should be understood that this is the worship of the congregation and not
just of the family involved, and a complete service should be
planned as close to the norm as possible.

The water used should be common water, as it is the act of
God that makes even the common sacred. To use special water, such as water imported from the Holy Land, is to obscure
the meaning of God's action and to risk investing the sacrament with superstitious overtones. It also suggests that one
baptized with "special" water has received something more
than others. Such a practice is to be avoided.

When infants are baptized, it has become customary for
the minister to hold the child. The parents or guardians give
the child to the minister, symbolizing their dedication of the
child to God; the minister represents the whole church in
embracing the child, indicating the welcome of the church
and the future nurture to be provided.

Following baptism, the baptized person is blessed with the
laying on of hands, which indicates that baptism is the "basic
ordination" of all Christians. The person may be anointed (it
may be an option for the baptized person or family), which
signifies that the baptized belongs to Christ ("Christ" literally
means "Anointed One") and is marked as a member of the
Body of Christ, the church. Anointing will not obscure or
supplant the act of baptizing with water. Anointing is simply
a visible symbol and is not a necessary or integral part of
baptism.

Traditionally baptism is the occasion for bestowing the
"Christian name" on a person. This is in recognition of the
fact that God knows us each personally and calls us by name
to be followers of Jesus Christ. Furthermore, it is a way of
indicating that our personal identity is connected to our iden-

tity as God's person. We are who we are by the grace of God. Therefore, the name of the one baptized should be clearly announced as part of the service.

In some churches, the one baptized is presented to the congregation. A child may be carried into the midst of the people and an adult so escorted, as a way of introducing and welcoming the new disciple.

A candle may be lighted at the beginning of the baptismal order as a sign of the presence of Christ who is the Light of the World. The baptismal candle should be lighted from the candle representing Christ.

The Holy Spirit plays a vital role in baptism, for it is by the power of the Spirit that the grace of God is claimed. Common water becomes, by the blessing of the Holy Spirit, a fountain of deliverance and rebirth. The Spirit then washes away the sins and raises to new life the one baptized. We pray in baptism not only that the Spirit will bless the water but that the Spirit will be poured out as well on the one baptized.

The prayers used in baptism remind us of God's deliverance by water in the Bible. Noah and his family were preserved in the ark upon the flood, and this ancient story has been noted as a prototype of Christian baptism. The deliverance of the people of Israel through the Red Sea is also understood as prefiguring Christian baptism.

Baptism is the sacrament of unity. While there is division among Christians about how we may celebrate the Lord's Supper together, baptism is all but universally accepted by Christian denominations. There may be local opportunities to share in baptisms with a church of a different denomination, Protestant, Roman Catholic, Anglican, or Orthodox. It is possible for members of one congregation to be present for baptisms in another, having a visible and even verbal part in the ceremony, as a way of signaling that baptism is into the universal church and not into a single denomination. (*See also* Affirmation of Faith; Anointing; Baptism, Infant and Believer; Candles; Confession of Faith; Cross, Sign of; Easter Vigil; Font, Baptismal; Holy Spirit; Laying on of Hands; Lent;

Renewal of Baptism; Renunciation of Evil; Resurrection; Sacrament; Salvation History.)

Baptism, Infant and Believer.

There are not two baptisms but one. It is clear that the person who comes for baptism is claimed by God on God's initiative. There are, in a real sense, no volunteers for God's service: all are conscripted. We are chosen by God not because of any merit or example of faith on our part but because God chooses us in spite of our lack of qualifications. This is clearest when it is an infant being baptized, brought to the church in the arms of another. It is just as true when an adult is baptized. Any adult who comes forward for baptism should realize that he or she is the recipient of God's unmerited grace and does nothing to qualify for entrance into the church.

The church has apparently baptized infants from early times. Whole families were baptized into the new Christian faith, including children. The Protestant Reformers for the most part continued this practice, finding it consistent with New Testament theology. Children are understood to be very much a part of the Christian family and are expected to be at the family meal at the Lord's Table in most denominations.

Some Protestant traditions hold a contrasting view and baptize only adults. Here there is the conviction that one must be able to respond affirmatively to the grace of God by making a commitment of personal faith. Therefore, baptizing infants is seen as inappropriate, and an adult making a profession of faith would be baptized regardless of whether the person had been baptized as an infant.

Many Protestants baptize adults who have not been previously baptized but stress the baptism of infants. There is a realization that baptism is the beginning of one's life in Christ and will issue in personal commitment, witness, and service. For the infant, this means a commitment on the part of the church to nurture the child in faith toward personal confession of faith and a life of discipleship. For the adult, this means a similar commitment on the church's part to help the disciple grow in faith and in service. Baptism in either case is prophetic of the Christian life, the beginning of a long process to be developed through one's life by the church.

In baptizing infants and adults, a "magical" application of the sacrament is to be avoided. Sometimes parents will want a child baptized as a means of insuring salvation or guaranteeing admission to heaven. Such an approach attempts to manipulate God to get something one wants. Baptism, to the contrary, is a recognition that God claims our lives to be and do what God wants. Adults sometimes, too, in times of severe crisis or approaching death will ask for baptism as a guarantee of salvation rather than as a recognition of God's total claim on that person's life. (*See also* Affirmation of Faith; Baptism; Confession of Faith.)

Baptism of the Lord.

The Sunday after Epiphany is celebrated as the Baptism of the Lord (see Mark 1:4–11). The baptism of Jesus by John the Baptist in the Jordan River marks the inauguration of Jesus' ministry. This day continues the Epiphany emphasis on the manifestation of Jesus as the Christ of God, even though the day is technically in ordinary time. The color for Sundays following Epiphany is green except for this day. Because it is a feast of Jesus Christ, the color is white.

The Baptism of the Lord is a time to remember that in baptism we are claimed by Christ to share in his ministry. It is, therefore, a day to renew the baptismal vows that bind us in covenant with God and to reaffirm our commitment as disciples of the risen Christ.

The baptism of Jesus by John is not the same as our baptisms. The baptism offered by John was a call to repentance, to a renunciation of sin, and a change of one's life direction from evil toward God. While this is applicable to our baptisms, it obviously does not apply to Jesus Christ. The baptism of Jesus brings another dimension to our baptisms, namely the promise of God's power in the descent of the

Holy Spirit. Therefore, as we remember that we are claimed by Christ and made one with Christ in baptism, so we remember that we are empowered by the Holy Spirit to carry out our ministry as disciples of Jesus Christ. (_See also_ Baptism; Renewal of Baptism.)

Baptismal Font.

See Font, Baptismal.

Benediction.

The benediction is a blessing (and is sometimes called "the blessing") pronounced on God's behalf by the minister of Word and sacrament to the people of God. It has its origins in the Aaronic benediction (Num. 6:23–27) and the apostolic benediction (2 Cor. 13:13). A benediction is a reminder of our being blessed by the grace of God, which moves us to bless God in our praise and the practice of our faith in the world.

Often coupled with a "charge" to the people, sending them forth to serve the Lord, the benediction is a blessing that reminds them of the power of the Holy Spirit given by God to accomplish what they are charged to do.

The benediction in Protestant churches is a brief action having antecedents in a much fuller ritual of the Middle Ages that included the presentation of the consecrated bread visually as a blessing on the people. Since this practice was derived from a Western custom of reserving the consecrated bread that the Reformers found repugnant, all suggestions of it are absent in Protestant worship. The blessed bread contains no inherent power to bless people; such a notion was considered superstitious. Nevertheless, the Reformers retained for the clergy the "priestly" function of pronouncing the benediction. They understood ministers to be ordained in the tradition of the apostles. Therefore those who are ordained as ministers of Word and sacrament, who preach and preside at the Lord's Table, are also the ones to pronounce the apostolic benediction. These are the particular responsibilities of the clergy by virtue of their ordination and neither result from nor confer any status of privilege or piety. Because it is the minister's function to preach and preside at the Table, the pronouncing of the benediction is the minister's as well since the benediction is a reminder of the promises of grace given in scripture and sacrament. The benediction is, therefore, the final blessing given to the people as they go into the world, a reminder of the blessing of God's Word received in sermon and sacrament. (*See also* Blessing; Minister; Mission; Ordination.)

Benedictus.

See Canticle.

Bible/Scripture/Word of God.

The Bible stands at the center of Christian worship. The early Christians used what we call the Old Testament in its Greek translation (the Septuagint or LXX) and read passages in their worship, followed by a sermon. Thus they followed the pattern of synagogue worship. Later, known as the service of the Word, this comprised the first of two parts of Christian worship, the second part being the service of the Lord's Supper. When the original apostles died, writings believed to have been composed by them and those that carried their authority were collected and added to the biblical readings in church. Eventually these were sorted out by usage and debate, and an authoritative list, called the *canon* (from a Latin word meaning "rule" or "standard"), was compiled.

In the Bible Christians discovered the Word of God spoken in Jesus Christ. When we say that the Bible is "the Word of God," what we mean is not that the Bible is itself dictated by God word-for-word but that the Bible contains and expresses the Word of God, which is Jesus Christ. Therefore, it is in the reading and hearing of scripture that we believe that the risen Christ comes to be present with those gathered in his name, just as we believe Christ is present to us in the sacraments.

Because the Bible presents to us the living Christ, the Bible itself becomes a testimony to Christ's Lordship, calling us to faithfulness and right living as disciples. In this sense the Bible becomes a standard by which faith and practice are measured. The authority of scripture is nothing less than the authority of the crucified and risen Jesus Christ. In worship disciples come to hear God's Word for them and to stand under that authority for their lives.

The preacher, no less than others, stands under the authority of scripture and is obligated to listen before daring to speak that word. The preacher, then, becomes the agent by which the Word of God may be communicated to the people of God. It is not the preacher's authority but the authority of the Word that matters. The preacher preaches from scripture, expounding the Word of God rather than airing personal opinions.

All of worship stands under the authority of scripture. We are not free to worship any way we want. On the contrary, we are to worship in response to God's Word spoken in Jesus Christ. Even our worship, therefore, is accountable to the authority of scripture.

This does not mean that we must adopt a rigid biblicism, nor should we worship the Bible. Nevertheless, the Bible is itself a vehicle for the communication of the Word, Jesus Christ. As such, the Bible contains many expressions of prayer and praise that are useful models for our worship. The Bible provides no definitive instructions about worship, however, and what we do find there must be transposed into a modern context. The mere use of biblical texts in worship is no guarantee of biblical worship but may even degenerate into a form of bibliolatry that can distract from the worship of God.

The custom in many Christian churches is to read several passages of scripture each Lord's Day. There is ordinarily a reading from the Old Testament, followed by a congregational response in the singing or saying of a Psalm; a reading from the New Testament, usually from one of the epistles; and finally a reading from a Gospel. (Notice that the Psalter selection is not technically a "reading" of scripture but a

scriptural response by the congregation to the first reading.)
The use of three readings from scripture is a way of allowing
the Word to be heard in full voice. A principle of biblical
study affirmed by the Reformers was that "scripture inter-
prets scripture." When a sufficient selection is read, then
something of the context of a given text becomes apparent.
The sermonic emphasis is understood in relation to the fuller
expression of the Word of God in scripture.

The placement of the Bible in the worship space suggests
something of the attitude of the worshipers toward the Bible.
A *central pulpit* witnesses to the centrality of the Word of
God. When the Bible is open on the pulpit, it is a sign that the
preacher should be expounding the Word of God rather than
human wisdom. Such an arrangement allows for the sermon
to come immediately following the reading of scripture. A
divided chancel with a lectern on one side and a pulpit on
the other communicates something different. It is designed to
show that preaching is not of the same authority as scripture.
Preaching the Word is subject to the authority of the biblical
witness to the Word.

Many different English translations and paraphrases are
available for reading in worship, and care should be given to
their selection. Some are particularly easy to read and understand (*Today's English Version*, for example) but may leave
something to be desired as translations since they simplify
the language to the point that precision in translation is lost.
Others are excellent scholarly translations (*New English
Bible, Jerusalem Bible*) but are not always easy to read or
listen to. *The King James Version*, for all its eloquence, is
difficult to read with meaning, and its sound, though melodi-
ous, is strange to modern ears. The safest versions for use in
worship are the *Revised Standard Version* and especially the
more recent *New Revised Standard Version*. The lector
should be cautious about selecting other versions that may be
paraphrases rather than proper translations (*The Living Bible*, J. B. Phillips) since they tend to interpretation rather than
proclamation. (*See also* Language of Worship; Lectern;

Preaching/Proclaiming the Word; Psalter; Pulpit; Service for
the Lord's Day.)

Bidding Prayer.

A *bidding prayer* is one in which the leader "bids" or asks
the people to pray for a certain subject, usually to offer intercessions for specific people. Bidding prayers come in a group
and often take the form of a litany, that is they include a set
response after each prayer. The sequence might be as follows:

The leader says "Let us pray for . . . " (noting the people
in need, such as "the sick").

A time of silent prayer in which the people offer personal
prayers for people with that need, either generally or by
name.

A summary prayer by the leader (concluding with, e.g.,
"Lord, in your mercy").

A response by the people (e.g., "Hear our prayer").

Then the sequence is repeated with a different need or
subject.

Bidding prayers involve the worshipers in several ways.
First, they call attention to the needs of others. They also
allow the worshipers to be specific in personal silent prayer.
Finally, the people respond in unison, indicating their soli-
darity in the concern for which prayer is offered. (*See also*
Intercession; Prayer.)

Blessing.

The "blessing" is often thought of as a prayer said at meal-
time and as such reflects the relationship of all meals to the
Lord's Supper. At the Last Supper, Jesus took, blessed, broke,
and gave bread. The blessing was a prayer to bless God for the
grace of God that provides sustenance of life. This prayer,
however, blesses the bread or the meal as well, recognizing
that in the food we receive a gift from God.

The term "blessing" is also applied to the benediction

pronounced at the end of a worship service. (*See also* Benediction.)

Bread/Wine.

Bread and wine are the elements used in celebrating the sacrament of the Lord's Supper. They are physical objects that help us to be in touch with the invisible presence of Christ. Bread and wine are signs of our human limitation and thus speak of God's incarnation in Jesus Christ. As God came in the physical person of Jesus Christ, so God comes by physical means again to be present in our world today.

Bread and wine are common elements with which we are familiar in our daily lives. The bread and wine do not speak of God, but the Holy Spirit opens our eyes to recognize Christ present in the breaking of bread and the sharing of the wine. The elements themselves are only vehicles by which God shares Jesus Christ. The fact that the bread and wine are shared is significant. As God's life was shared with us in Jesus Christ, so we share that same life in eating and drinking.

Bread. Jesus referred to himself as the Bread of Life (John 6:35–65) and in breaking the bread at the Last Supper indicated that it was indeed his body. Bread signifies what is basic to life, the common source of nourishment and subsistence. Jesus Christ is our bread, the basic element of our nourishment and growth in faith. Christ is the one we all have in common; Christ is the source of our unity.

The body of Christ was broken on the cross in the sharing of God's love for the world. So it is that we break bread in order to share it. It is helpful if the communion bread is in the form of a loaf (or at least loaves) so that it may be broken and shared among the people. Cubed or diced bread or wafers tend to emphasize an individualistic approach to communion.

Wine. The cup of wine played an important part in the Last Supper as it did in the ancient Passover meal. In both cases it became a sign of the covenant between God and the people, a covenant that was to be sealed once and for all with the blood of Christ. The cup is to be shared by all the people as they reaffirm their common covenant relationship with God.

The use of a common cup, from which all drink, is an appropriate way to signal the people's sharing in the covenant. Using individual cups may seem to work against the sense of common covenant. In practice, however, a single cup from which all drink is rarely used; several chalices may be required to serve a congregation. Using trays of individual cups, therefore, may be understood as an extension of that practice. The commonality of covenantal sharing is expressed not in the size of the cup but in the act of serving one another.

The use of fermented wine presents some problems. Grape juice has been accepted as a substitute in many churches since the temperance movement in the nineteenth and early twentieth century. Some suggest that using grape juice is inaccurate and that only fermented wine should be used since that is what Jesus used. Others argue that unfermented grape juice is rightfully included in the biblical definition of wine. The incidence of alcoholism in our culture today requires a new look at the use of fermented wine. Questions are raised whether its use prevents alcoholics from coming to the Table and whether it is appropriate for children to receive. Some have found it helpful to have both fermented and unfermented available at a given service, with each clearly identified by notice in the bulletin. Such a practice will display sensitivity to the needs of the people. (*See also* Chalice and Plate; Holy Spirit; Lord's Supper; Offering.)

Breaking of Bread.

See Lord's Supper.

Bulletin.

Most congregations print up a bulletin including basic information about the congregation, the order of service, and announcements about current concerns and activities of the faith community. The bulletin is, therefore, a tangible sum-

mary of the community that is the church in that congregation. It may give helpful information regarding pastors and
leaders of the church and their availability to members and
newcomers. Some churches, for instance, list the members of
the governing board along with names of pastors, educators,
and musicians. Phone numbers of the church office and key
people might also be included.

The use of graphic art in the bulletin offers an opportunity
to display symbols that may be helpful to the worshiper in
anticipating the worship service. Seasonal symbols inform
the worshiper, upon entering, about what will be happening
in the service. Other symbols may illustrate the scriptural or
sermonic emphasis. Sometimes a picture of the church building is used on the cover, but this is an inadequate definition
of who the congregation is because it identifies the church as
property.

The order of service printed in the bulletin provides a kind
of road map for the journey of worship. Awareness of the
service's structure is helpful to the worshiper in that it provides a certain sense of security. There are those who argue
against the use of a printed order for this very reason, for it
seems to work against freedom and spontaneity in worship.
Nevertheless, if the printed order is used as a guide, not an
authority, it may be helpful in showing the direction of worship without spelling out all details. It gives the worshiper a
sense of journey throughout the service and a confidence in
being led.

The announcements in print will minimize verbal announcements in the course of the service. Announcements
that apply to groups of the congregation may be printed (and
thus be informative to everyone) without using everyone's
time to speak of matters of primary concern to only a few.

The bulletin should be printed in black on light colored
paper. Some colored inks are particularly difficult for some
people to read (blue, for example, being one of the worst). If
the church owns a copier with capability to enlarge, it is helpful to have a few large-print versions available for those who

need them. Attached to each should be enlarged copies of the
hymns for that day. A notice should appear in the bulletin, in
enlarged type, announcing the availability of the large-print
bulletins. (*See also* Announcements; Art; Service for the
Lord's Day; Symbols.)

Call to Worship.

The call to worship is the summons to praise God at the
opening of the service and is sometimes termed "Sentences of
Scripture." It is usually taken from scripture for two reasons:
we are summoned by the Word revealed in scripture, and
only words of scripture are appropriate to call us to the worship of Almighty God. In either case the point is the same:
We are summoned by God to worship. It is at God's initiative
that we come, not ours.

The call to worship is similar to the introit, which may be
defined as a sung call to worship, usually sung by the choir.
However, a call to worship may also be sung. When it is, the
congregation joins in the singing.

The call to worship is often sung or said responsively, that
is, in dialogue between the worship leader and the people.
This dialogue involves the congregation in responding to
God's call immediately and acknowledges the community
that is established by God's call. (*See also* Congregation; Procession; Service for the Lord's Day.)

Candles.

Candles were probably first used in worship for practical
rather than liturgical purposes. Among early Christians, the
evening prayer service or vigil required candles for illumination. Candles soon carried a symbolic content as well. As
darkness approached and a candle was lighted, surely worshipers recalled the verse referring to Jesus Christ: "The light
shines in the darkness, and the darkness did not overcome it"
(John 1:5). The evening candle then represented the Easter
candle and pointed to Christ's resurrection. In this way, can-

dles have a liturgical function in showing the light of Christ's salvation versus the encroachment of darkness (see Isa. 9:2 and John 8:12).

We who follow Christ are to be lights as well, and the lighting of candles reminds us of our responsibilities to be "the light of the world" commanded by Christ (at Mt. 5:14–16). In some traditions, individuals light candles as an act of faith, signifying personal commitment and concern in the offering of prayer.

Two candles are often used to represent Christ, indicating Christ's dual nature, human and divine. Such candles are often placed on either side of a cross. Candles flanking a pulpit or lectern similarly indicate that the human-divine Christ is the Word revealed in scripture. The candles give illumination, literally and figuratively, to the proclamation of God's Word (Christ) from the Bible.

Sometimes a special candle represents Christ's presence. This Christ candle (or Paschal candle) may be regularly present in worship or may find particular use during special services such as the Easter Vigil.

Candles can do much to create an atmosphere of quiet meditation in worship, especially at evening or night services. Even in the daytime, candles suggest the presence of Christ. The odor of burning candles can make a strong subjective impression on the worshiper who associates candles with prayer, the presence of Christ, and the atmosphere of worship. (*See also* Easter Vigil; Paschal Candle; Procession.)

Canticle.

The term *canticle* comes from a Latin word meaning "little song." It usually refers to biblical songs other than the Psalms.

The most commonly used canticles in Christian worship are Mary's Song (the Magnificat, Luke 1:46–55), Zechariah's Song (the Benedictus, Luke 1:68–79), and Simeon's Song (the Nunc Dimittis, Luke 2:29–32). Since these were apparently intended to be sung, musical settings are available in many modern hymnals and prayer books. These canticles are firmly set by tradition to be used in Morning, Evening, and Night Prayer each day.

There are other biblical songs, such as the Song of Moses (Exod. 15:1–18 and Deut. 32:1–43), the Song of Hannah (1 Sam. 2:1–10—compare with the Song of Mary), and the Song of Isaiah (Isaiah 12) in the Old Testament, and in the New Testament the Song of Christ's Self-giving (Phil. 2:5–11) and the Song of Christ's Nature (Col. 1:15–20).

These and other examples of biblical songs remind us that God's people have always sung their prayers and praises. These texts still provide us language for our sung worship. If musical settings for any of these texts are not readily available, they can be easily sung as chants with congregational responses. (*See also* Chant; Daily Prayer.)

Cantor.

See Musician.

Carol.

A carol is a particular kind of song. It has its origins in European folk music, particularly in France, Germany, and England. It is characterized by a tune that is rhythmic and easy to sing and a text that contains a refrain. Carols are related to ballads and dance tunes, and were probably used for dances and processions during the Middle Ages. Carols are most often associated with Christmas because of their sprightly and celebrative nature.

At the time of the Reformation, carols were not composed in Protestant circles, probably because of the austere view the Reformers had about the Roman liturgy. By that time the carol had become established as an art form in the church, and musicians were writing and composing them. Their popularity has persisted, and carols are sung in a variety of ethnic and national traditions.

Carols are recognizable today by their popular appeal. They are simple and singable, enjoyed by people in shopping malls and churches alike. Because they are easily learned, they are sung readily in informal gatherings as well as used liturgically. They contribute enormously to the repertoire of the people's music as well as to their theological understanding. (*See also* Dance; Hymn; Procession.)

Chalice and Plate (Paten).

The word *chalice* comes from a Latin word meaning simply "cup," but it has come to be applied primarily to a vessel used at celebrations of the Lord's Supper. Often such vessels are ornate in decoration and design, made of precious metals, and sometimes even set with jewels out of honor and respect for Jesus Christ. Protestant churches generally use more simply designed chalices, but these too are finely crafted from precious metals. At the Last Supper, however, it is most likely that Jesus used an ordinary drinking cup as well as a common household plate for the bread.

The chalice was an object of reverence in the Middle Ages as people viewed it from a distance. Because Christ was understood to be present in either the bread or the wine, it was not necessary for the cup to be given to the people, so it could be withheld from the laity as an expression of clerical domination and control. Since lay people did not drink from the cup, the use of the chalice became essentially symbolic and ceremonial. Since only the priest drank from it, the cup was relatively small. The Protestant Reformation insisted that the wine be offered to the people once again, and the need for a larger cup became apparent.

In many Protestant churches, a common cup is not used. A chalice is used ceremonially only by the presiding minister. The people (and usually the minister too) drink from small individual cups served in trays. A common cup may be used for a small group. Several chalices are generally provided for the people in most Roman Catholic services. Orthodox churches, which have always given the cup to the people, do so by placing bread in the cup and using a small spoon to transmit the wine-soaked morsel of bread into the mouth of the communicant. Many churches practice another form of intinction: the minister or each person dips the bread into the wine or grape juice in the chalice.

Accompanying the chalice is the *paten,* or plate. Though the Lord's Supper was related to the Passover when unleavened bread was used, the early Christians celebrated it more often at other times in the context of a fellowship meal when leavened bread would have been used. Leavened bread was most commonly used for the sacrament for the first thousand years, and the plate was large enough to accommodate loaves, probably more the size of a tray. This large plate was used to collect the people's offerings of their bread from home (associating the offering plate, therefore, with the communion service) and for the serving of the consecrated bread to the people. Only in the West did the bread take the form of a small wafer, which resulted in smaller plates that often double as covers for the chalices. In many Protestant churches, several plates are used to distribute the bread (usually leavened) among the people. (*See also* Bread/Wine; Lord's Supper.)

Chancel.

The term comes from a Latin word referring to the screens separating the area where the clergy were from the rest of the church. In modern usage, therefore, it refers to that part of the worship space where the clergy and other worship leaders are, including the choir if it is located in front of the congregation. In the chancel area one usually also finds the pulpit, the table, and perhaps the baptismal font.

The distinction of the chancel as the area reserved for the clergy is not as widely made today as in the past. The participation of lay readers of scripture and others in various leadership roles has effectively taken down the dividers. Even in Orthodox churches, the rood screen separating the chancel area has been opened up so the people can participate at least by watching the priest. Still, the term chancel is applied to that portion of the room that becomes the focal center of the worship space. (*See also* Choir; Font, Baptismal; Pulpit; Table.)

Chant.

Chanting is a way to sing a prose text. Most words written to be sung have particular poetic cadences, meters, forms, or rhymes that accommodate musical rhythms and structures. Chanting, on the other hand, allows a prose text to be sung according to the rhythms and emphases of normal speech. Speaking, rather than music, carries the meaning. The text need not be forced into other structures but may remain in its spoken form.

Chanting is particularly helpful in singing biblical texts, primarily the Psalms, which were intended to be sung but which come to us in an English form that resembles prose more than what we commonly think of as poetry. Those Protestants who have been particularly noted as Psalm-singers, such as the Presbyterians and Episcopalians, have confronted this problem in essentially two ways. One significant contribution has been the metrical psalm. The prose text is retranslated into modern poetic form with meter and rhyme, and then set to one or more tunes. In some Protestant traditions, another means of singing the Psalms has also been preserved, namely chanting.

In chanting "tones" are set, simple melodies with one or more sustaining notes on which most of a line is sung. Because the sustaining tone can be of any length, the melodic line can accommodate few or many syllables. The Gloria Patri, for example, is usually sung to an Old Scottish chant. Many other examples are to be found in modern hymnals, and chant tones are provided in Lutheran, Episcopal, Roman Catholic, and Presbyterian resources by which any Psalm or other prose texts may be sung.

The effect of chanting a prose text is that it lengthens the syllables and slows the pace of the words, giving more time for comprehension and contemplation. Singing enhances the emphases of the spoken words, and a variety of tones is available to give different feelings appropriate to different texts. While the chanting is often done by soloists or choirs, it can be done effectively by a congregation. In any case, most chant tones provide a refrain that may be sung by all when the verse is chanted by one or a few. (*See also* Canticles; Psalms.)

Charge.

See Benediction; Mission.

Charism/Charisma/Charismatic.

Charism comes from a Greek word meaning a gift freely and graciously given. In Christian usage it refers to a gift of grace from God. Charisms (or charismata) are gifts or talents perceived to be divinely inspired. One who has a gift for preaching the gospel, for instance, may be said to have a charism. Paul, in Romans 12:6 notes that we have "gifts" that differ according to the grace God bestows, and in 1 Corinthians 12:4, he notes that we have different "gifts" in the same Spirit. In both instances, and elsewhere, the word for "gifts" is *charismata* or charisms. Charisms are given not for the benefit of the person so gifted but that the gift might be shared in the service and to the glory of God.

One who displays charisms, God's special gifts, is one who has "charisma." This word has gained currency in modern English, used in reference to political and public figures. One who has "charisma" in this sense displays an attractiveness that draws popular allegiance. In the Christian sense, charisma is better understood as an indication that a person is blessed by God's gifts rather than a measure of popularity. Usually the possessor of charisma is modest about his or her gifts and oblivious to any personal adulation that may result. That person recognizes that the gifts are by God's grace and are to be used in God's service, not for personal status.

Charismatic refers to those who understand God to have blessed them with particular charisms or gifts to be used in the service of Jesus Christ, often speaking in tongues or prophesying. In a broader sense, charismatic refers to a style of worship that is highly participatory and vocal. Leaders and worshipers experience charisms of speaking in tongues or prophetic utterances, for example, as well as a variety of other ministries to benefit others, all of which are affirmed as being empowered by the Holy Spirit. The charismatic worshiper is frequently overwhelmed by a sense of the presence of the Spirit, and the vocal and physical expressions of joy and praise (such as dancing) are signs of the charism. All of this takes place primarily in the community of God's people; it is not just a private or individual ecstatic experience. The gifts of the Spirit cannot be earned or self-induced in any way; they are pure and free gifts from God. (*See also* Ecstatic Utterances/Speaking in Tongues; Holy Spirit.)

Chasuble.

See Vestments/Robes/Stoles.

Choir.

The use of a choir in worship dates back to the Old Testament Temple. The Book of Psalms suggests there was singing back and forth between groups of people, probably sections of a choir.

Choirs became prevalent in Christian churches in the fourth century when churches became legal and worship more public. In order to assure the highest quality of music offered up in praise of God, it eventually became desirable to have people set apart for a special ministry of song in worship, just as had been done by the ancient Jews.

In the Middle Ages, complex and intricate music was sung by the choir, while simple refrains and easy melodies were left to the congregation. The Reformation shifted the purpose of the choir somewhat. The choir's reason for existence was not primarily to perform music too elaborate or difficult for a congregation but to assist the congregation in its singing. Luther gave the chorale to the people and Calvin the metrical psalm so that the congregation would participate more fully in the music of worship. Both used choirs to encourage

and enhance the congregation's participation. They understood the choir not as a surrogate for the congregation but as
its leader.

The true choir in Christian worship is the congregation.
All God's people come to praise God and do so in song. In
any fellowship of Christians there are those who are blessed
with lovely voices, and these are set apart in an auxiliary
choir, representatives of the congregation who devote time
and energy to prepare for singing in worship. The work of the
choir is twofold: first, to prepare musical offerings to inspire
and uplift the people in their worship, and second, to rehearse the congregation's parts—hymns, responses, refrains,
and doxologies—to support and lead the people in their
singing.

Every choir must remember that it is not performing before the congregation. What it does is praise God on behalf
of the congregation. It is important, therefore, that a choir
maintain an attitude of prayer in its rehearsals as well as in
its offerings during a service. The choir needs to remember
that it is singing to worship God, first and foremost. Its
prayer is always that its music will serve to bring others
closer to God.

The choir may be placed in the worship space in several
ways, each having advantages and disadvantages. Having the
choir face the congregation in the chancel area offers an intimate and personal atmosphere as choir and congregation sur-
round the table. The disadvantage lies in that the choir
appears to be "on stage" and is easily enticed into performing
for the congregation. In a divided chancel some of this may
be avoided if the choir faces across the line of vision of the
congregation when singing by itself, and turns toward the
congregation when supporting the singing of the people. Lo-
cating the choir behind the congregation avoids the problem
of performance and emphasizes the choir's support for congregational singing. However, when the choir is singing by
itself or in dialogue with the congregation, hearing voices
without seeing people can be distracting and disconcerting.
Placing the choir to one side of the main body of the congre-

gation has the advantage of not being on display but the possible disadvantage of acoustical difficulties. Seating the choir as part of the congregation will encourage congregational singing but may be awkward in other respects.

The choir performs a vital role in Christian worship not only in leading the congregation in its singing but in preserving great music of the church's heritage and in introducing music by contemporary authors and composers. Christian liturgy is alive and dynamic, and the choir makes a significant contribution to its vitality. (*See also* Chancel; Congregation; Musician.)

Christ the King.

Christ the King Sunday is the last Sunday of the Christian year, the Sunday just before Advent when the annual cycle begins again. This day is a summary of the whole year. Christ is worshiped as sovereign ruler over all creation, nations, and peoples. Christ's rule is one of peace and justice. Christ is the One who claims our highest loyalty.

Since this is a festival of the Lord, the appropriate color is white. (*See also* Christian Year.)

Christian Year (Liturgical Calendar).

The church has devised its own calendar over the course of the centuries. The Christian Year has regular seasons and special days, which provide a rhythm for the worship of Christians gathered into congregations. Also known as the Liturgical Calendar, this schedule is a way of marking chronological time by celebrating God's mighty acts in Jesus Christ.

The life of Jesus is the basis for the Christian calendar. We come together at God's call to worship in the name of Jesus Christ, and we recall what God has done and is doing in this world. In our worship we methodically rehearse the life of Christ so we can better be Christ's disciples.

The Christian Year has its roots in the Bible. By the power of the Holy Spirit, the Bible is for us the unique and authoritative witness to Christ in the life of the church. Through the course of the year the whole biblical story of Jesus Christ and the people of God is told in our worship.

The Christian Year is arranged around two major festivals: Christmas and Easter. Each is preceded by a season of preparation. Each also begins a season that climaxes in a special day. Other special days are also observed along the way, filling out the story of Jesus Christ. The periods designated "ordinary time" are simply not in any special season.

The basic structure of the Christian Year is shown in the left column with other special days listed in the right column:

Advent (4 Sundays)	Christmas Eve
Christmas Day/ Season	(12 days)
Epiphany (1 day)	Baptism of the Lord (Sunday after Epiphany)
Ordinary Time	Transfiguration (Sunday before Lent)
Lent (40 weekdays)	Ash Wednesday Holy Week Palm/Passion Sunday Maundy Thursday Good Friday Easter Vigil
Easter Day/Season (50 days)	Ascension (40 days after Easter)
Pentecost (1 day)	Trinity (Sunday after Pentecost)
Ordinary Time	All Saints' Day (Nov.1) Christ the King Sunday (Sunday before Advent)

(*See also* Church Year; Ordinary Time; Season.)

Christmas.

Christmas Eve. In the biblical way of reckoning time, still observed by Jews today, each day is said to begin at sundown. Days are so noted in the creation story—"And there was evening and there was morning, the first day" (Gen. 1:5). The eve of a special day, therefore, may be thought of as the beginning of the day itself. On the other hand, it also concludes the time of preparation for that day. Both emphases come together in times like Christmas Eve and Easter Vigil, days that culminate periods of preparation and begin the celebrations themselves.

Christmas Eve, then, is the transition between the season of Advent and the day of Christmas. This celebration summarizes the themes of Advent—longing, prophecy, and preparation—and leads into the fullness of rejoicing of Christmas Day. Many people do not attend church on Christmas Day itself unless it falls on a Sunday. This makes the Christmas Eve celebration even more important as a time to begin emphasis on Christmas themes, which will be amplified on the Sundays following Christmas.

Christmas Day/Season. The nativity of Jesus Christ, Christmas, is the celebration of God's entering human history in the person of Jesus of Nazareth. Advent expectations are fulfilled in the celebrations of Christmas. The longings and hopes expressed in Advent are met by God's taking human form and identifying with sinful humankind. God is with us, in person, in the flesh, incarnate, and we are moved to worship God in the hush of awe and the gladness of deep joy.

December 25 was appropriated as the date for Christmas by the church in the fourth century. The actual date of Christ's birth is unknown, but December 25 seemed fitting because that was near the winter solstice, when the sun begins to move north along the horizon and daylight begins to increase in the northern hemisphere. The coming of Jesus Christ, the Sun of Righteousness and the Light of the World, was naturally associated with this date, and the secular festival was filled with Christian content. Some Christians, however, have downplayed Christmas because of its early association with pagan festivals.

Christmas as a season goes beyond Christmas day to the twelve days leading to Epiphany. This indicates that Christmas is not a momentary celebration but one that requires a period of meditation and reflection on the mystery of God's incarnation. The church is at odds with the secular calendar at this point, for public holiday observances of the season are usually held in advance of Christmas, tending to preempt Advent and its preparations as well as discounting Christmas itself. The only antidote is to stress the full Christmas season by sustaining the celebrations through Epiphany. (*See also* Advent; Easter Vigil; Epiphany.)

Church Year.

The church year is a programmatic year in a local congregation, usually following the schedule of the local public school system. Beginning in September, the church year has a high level of activity that continues until summer when in many churches a simpler format is followed.

This term is sometimes applied to the Christian year, the calendar of worship celebrations. Conflicts may occur when the two are confused or the Christian year is forced to conform to the church year, when, for example, school vacations make it necessary to reschedule church observances, or when local stewardship emphases preempt Christ the King Sunday or Advent celebrations. In the life of a congregation, the church year should be subservient to the Christian year. (*See also* Christian Year.)

Collect.

A *collect* (pronounced coll'ect) is a particular form of a brief prayer. The origin of the term is uncertain, but it is thought to derive from the collecting of individual petitions into a terse summary form by the worship leader at different points during the service.

The term *collect* refers to a compact prayer with interdependent parts, following a classic pattern. The prayer begins with an *address to God*, simply naming the One to whom we pray, followed by an acknowledgment of certain *divine attributes* pertinent to the prayer's request. Then comes the *petition* itself, the core of the prayer that claims the promises of God inherent in the divine attributes just noted. This is the substantive part of the prayer. The petitioners remember also that they pray in the context of the full community of the church, the whole community of the people of God, and their prayers are on behalf of all. The prayer next indicates the *result desired* if the petition is granted and how the divine promises will be translated into the lives of the people. The final *doxology* praises Christ who is the mediator of our prayers to God.

Ancient prayers of this form invariably have the same structure, as does this modern example:

Address to God	Great God,
Divine Attributes	whose Son Jesus came as a servant among us:
Petition	control our wants and restrain our ambitions,
Result Desired	so that we may serve you faithfully and fulfill our lives;
Doxology	in Jesus Christ our Lord. Amen. (*Worshipbook*, p. 143.)

This simple structure is a helpful guide in formulating one's personal prayers as well as various prayers for worship, such as the prayer of the day. (*See also* God; Prayer; Prayer of the Day.)

Colors (Liturgical).

The use of color in the worship space is not simply for aesthetic purposes. In fact, color as decor alone might be a distraction from worship, calling attention to itself rather than to God who is the object of our worship. Liturgical colors, however, have an instructive purpose and are chosen to point us more clearly in God's direction.

It has become the tradition in various parts of the church to display certain colors for specific days and seasons as visual aids reminding worshipers of thematic emphases. The use of

the colors varies somewhat from time to time and from tradition to tradition. The following list reflects the customary
usage of many Christians today.

White represents purity and is used for all festivals of Jesus
Christ, primarily Christmas and Easter. It is also the color
used for All Saints' Day, signifying the purity of the white-
robed throng of redeemed people assembled before God's
throne (see Rev. 7:9–17).

Purple is used to suggest royalty, repentance, and even
suffering. During Lent, for example, the somberness of purple
reminds one of the need to be humble before God and hints
at the suffering that may come with following Christ. As the
color associated with royalty, it also points to Christ who
rules through suffering and sacrifice. A similar use of purple
is made during Advent, also a season of preparation and penitence similar to Lent, during which we await expectantly the
coming of the royal Christ.

Red also carries several meanings. At Pentecost, the color
red reflects the pentecostal fire of the Holy Spirit. On Good
Friday (or throughout Holy Week) it signifies the blood of
Christ, the Crucified One. Red may also be used to indicate
the royalty of Christ because at his mocking the soldiers put a
scarlet robe on him (Matt. 27:28). Red also signifies the blood
of the martyrs and is customarily used on days when people
who have died witnessing for the faith are remembered.

Green is used during those times of the year that are not in
any special season nor marked by any special day. Hence, the
period from Pentecost to the end of the year and the period
from Epiphany to the beginning of Lent use the color green.
It signifies growth, and during those times the church's worship focuses on themes of spiritual growth. It also signifies
the world, and during those times the church's worship lifts
up its global mission. It is an appropriate color for those
times between seasons.

White, purple, red, and green are the basic liturgical colors
and cover most days throughout the year. Other colors have
symbolic content and may be used from time to time:

Gold is a color that also suggests royalty and is appropriate at Christmas and Epiphany. As a symbol of the sun, gold may be used at Easter as well.

Blue suggests purity and hope. Associated with the Virgin Mary, it is often used during Advent and Christmas.

Black suggests mourning and is sometimes used on Ash Wednesday and Good Friday. The absence of any color has the same effect, as when all liturgical colors and decorations are removed for Good Friday.

Gray, the color of ashes, is appropriately used for Ash Wednesday.

Stoles, pulpit cloths, candles, and other accoutrements of worship may display these different colors and should be changed in accord with the change of seasons and special days in the church year. (*See also* Candles; Decorations; Season; Vestments/Stoles/Robes.)

Commendation.

See Funeral.

Committal.

See Funeral.

Communion.

See Lord's Supper.

Confession of Faith.

The confession of faith is the other side of the coin from the prayer of confession. We confess our faith in God, which makes it possible for us to approach God and confess sin. We believe this to be so because we are aware that in Jesus Christ God has approached us, overcome the separation of sin, and restored our broken relationship. Confessing this faith, we affirm God's grace in reestablishing unity with us.

A confession of faith is both timeless and timely. In our worship we affirm what God has done for our redemption in

Jesus Christ as we look for what God will do here and now. It is at once historical and personal. Each person is placed in the stream of history, each person is identified with the redemptive activity of Jesus Christ, and each person looks forward to the culmination of salvation history. A confession of faith is a personal and corporate commitment to the One in whom we believe, God revealed to us in Jesus Christ.

Examples of biblical confessions of faith include Deuteronomy 26:5–9 and 1 Corinthians 15:3–4. The Apostles' Creed (so called because it is a statement of the faith of the apostles, not because it is supposed to have been written by any of them) was probably originally a baptismal creed. While it is stated in the singular, it is meant to be used corporately, for in saying it we are united with the faith of the church from all ages. The Nicene Creed was written in response to a particular historical situation, as were other confessional statements prepared by Christians at different times.

The appropriate posture for making a confession of faith in worship is standing, out of reverence for the One in whom we trust for our salvation and to whom we subject ourselves in service.

The faith of the church is affirmed at the time of baptism by the whole church as well as by the one being baptized or by parents and sponsors. In this context it is usually referred to as an "affirmation of faith." The term "profession of faith" is usually applied to a personal public confession of faith by an individual upon baptism, confirmation, or joining the church. Another term sometimes used is "declaration of faith," although this most often refers to a document or formal confessional statement drawn up by a group of believers in a particular crisis situation. All, however, are confessions of faith. (*See also* Affirmation of Faith; Amen; Confession of Sin; Creed.)

Confession of Sin.

When we come before God in worship, one of the first things that happens is that we recognize our own smallness alongside God's greatness. If God is worthy of our worship, by comparison we are unworthy. The act of confession is a way in which we humans acknowledge our relationship with God as creatures before our Creator. What is more, confession is a liturgical act admitting that even that relationship is broken, that we are unrighteous before the Holy One. In confession we ask God, by the grace of forgiveness, to restore what is broken.

The Protestant Reformers rejected the medieval Roman Catholic Church's understanding of confession as a sacramental act, partly because it was not instituted by Christ and therefore could not rightly be termed a sacrament, and partly because it required the mediation of a priest. Protestants affirmed "the priesthood of all believers" as a way of understanding that the community of faith comes before God together and that Christ, who is present in the church, is the only mediator. Therefore confession was changed from a private act between a person and a priest to a public act by the congregation.

There are two forms of confession, general and personal. General confession is a prayer, often said in unison, that articulates commonly felt confessional needs. An example of this kind of prayer is found in Psalm 51, as well as in many modern liturgies. Personal confession finds a place in public worship in a time of silent prayer that may precede or follow the general confession. This observance is a reminder that all our personal prayer is in the context of the community of faith and never really private.

The prayer of confession helps prepare worshipers for hearing the Word of God proclaimed in scripture and sermon. In confession we recognize our own need for the healing and truth that God alone can give and does give in the Word, Jesus Christ. The act of confession, general and personal, makes us receptive to that Word. As the prayer of confession is preparation for the hearing of the Word, the confession of faith is our response to that Word. (*See also* Confession of Faith; Declaration of Forgiveness; Prayer.)

Confirmation (Commissioning).

Confirmation originated in the early centuries of the church as a ceremony that immediately followed baptism. It included a prayer by the bishop, anointing, laying on of hands, and making the sign of the cross. The word *confirmation* was understood in the sense of the bishop's ratification of what had been done in baptism.

The Reformers rejected this practice, affirming that baptism was itself sufficient and that confirmation as practiced in the Middle Ages was not instituted by Christ. Nevertheless, the Reformers required a profession of faith for one to be admitted to the Lord's Table, which in practice seemed more important than baptism, for it was at the Table that one entered upon full participation in the church. There was a need, then, for a liturgical opportunity for a person baptized as an infant to make a public profession of faith and enter personally into the covenant community. In modern times this act of admission to full church membership has been called confirmation. It is also commonly understood today in Protestant circles that the person confirms the vows made by someone else (parents, guardians, the church) at the time of his or her own baptism.

The "laying on of hands" is sometimes included in the Protestant confirmation ceremony but only as a blessing given the one confirmed and not to be considered as the completion of baptism. Viewing confirmation as the completion of baptism presents a problem since baptism does not come in two parts and does not require any other action, either by the one baptized or by the church's representative, to complete it. Confirmation is one's public acceptance of personal responsibility for one's baptism as one enters on a mature involvement in discipleship. One baptized as an infant will make a personal confession of faith, confirming the vows and promises made in baptism, by God, by the people of God, and by one's parents, accepting full responsibility in the community of faith. It is difficult to avoid perceiving confirmation as somehow completing baptism because of this connection.

In an attempt to resolve this problem, confirmation is sometimes coupled with or replaced by the term *commissioning*. This refers to the sending of the baptized and confirmed person on a mission for Christ. Commissioning indicates that the church, represented by the congregation, has a responsibility to send forth baptized Christians to fulfill their ministries as followers of Jesus Christ. This commissioning responsibility implies strongly the congregation's obligation to provide continued education, nurture, and support for those commissioned.

Both confirmation and commissioning are generally recognized as inadequate terms, and yet they continue to be used for want of any better ones. They present issues that are a continued source of discussion and even debate throughout the church. Confirmation was lifted out of a context integral to baptism and became understood as a completion of baptism. The church as a whole is struggling with healing the breech between baptism and confirmation. Commissioning is seen by many to be superfluous in that baptism itself commissions disciples. These matters will be on the agenda of ecumenical dialogue for some time to come. (*See also* Baptism; Confession of Faith; Laying on of Hands; Renewal of Baptism.)

Congregation.

The word *congregation* comes from Latin words meaning "gather together." A congregation in the ecclesiastical sense, then, is a gathering of people for religious purposes, specifically for worship. There is not, however, any suggestion that the gathering of the congregation is spontaneous on the part of the people. A congregation does not assemble on its own whim or even at its own pleasure. Rather it is gathered by God. Worship begins with a section of the liturgy sometimes called the gathering of God's people.

The Greek word for church (*ecclesia*, from which we get

our word "ecclesiastical") literally means "called out." The church is called out from the rest of the world to be God's peculiar people. In this sense, the congregation gathered for worship is called together by God, apart from the rest of the world, to be a unique people.

The congregation, as people called out by God to worship and serve God, is in a sense "exclusive." Those called by God have this particular purpose in a way that no one else does. At the same time, however, those called out by God are to come before God representing the whole world, and in this sense the congregation is "inclusive." The worship of the congregation gathers the needs of all people.

When we worship, we come together as people called by God, as the "call to worship" makes clear at the beginning of the service. The call to worship is usually in words of scripture, signifying that it is the Word of God who summons us to become a congregation at worship. By that Word we become a community of believers, and this is established at the beginning of the service.

The purpose of worship is to enable the congregation to praise God together, to join in prayers and songs, to listen together to the Word proclaimed in scripture, to celebrate the sacraments, and to make common commitment in response. Worship is a corporate act and requires a congregation. The Christian quorum is "two or three" (Matt. 18:20).

A congregation may be large or small, but it is always part of the fullness of the whole church of Jesus Christ of every denomination and sect. A congregation may also be understood as a parish, a local church, a geographical designation, but it is always a representation of the worldwide church of Jesus Christ. A congregation exists at a particular time, but it is always one with the church through all ages in the communion of saints. Any congregation at worship, then, exists in the context of a much larger body of people, all of whom are called by God to be the Body of Christ.

The Christian congregation primarily gathers on the Lord's Day (Sunday) to witness to the resurrection of the

Crucified One, Jesus Christ. While other special days and occasions are observed, this is the primary worship event. It is in this event that most people of a local church participate most of the time. Relatively few are involved in any other single activity of a congregation. (*See also* Call to Worship; Intercession; Service for the Lord's Day.)

Consecration.

See Institution, Words of.

Creed.

Our word *creed* comes from *credo*, which is Latin for "I believe." Creeds are associated with personal affirmations or professions of faith made by believers at baptisms.

The Apostles' Creed was originally such a statement of faith, given in question-and-answer form:

Do you believe in God the Father?
I believe in God, the Father almighty, creator of heaven and earth.
Do you believe in Jesus Christ, the Son of God?
I believe in Jesus Christ, his only Son, our Lord. . . .
Do you believe in God the Holy Spirit?
I believe in the Holy Spirit, the holy catholic Church. . . .

While a creedal affirmation is to be accepted personally and not uncritically adopted by an individual, it is also made in the context of the community of faith. (*See also* Affirmation of Faith; Amen; Confession of Faith.)

Cross.

The primary symbol of the Christian faith is the cross. For most Protestants, the cross is plain and simple. There are, however, many different styles of crosses.

In the early centuries of the church, the crucifixion was not represented in Christian art, probably because the early church saw the Christ-event in light of the resurrection. Only later in the Middle Ages did the church focus on the crucifix-

ion, which found artistic expression in such things as crucifixes. Crucifixes display a sculptured body, graphically
representing Christ crucified, most often used by Roman
Catholics, Episcopalians, and Lutherans.

Some crosses carry the letters "IHS," which some have
mistakenly assumed stands for *in hoc signo* referring to Con-
stantine's adoption of battle standards inscribed, *"In hoc
signo vinces"* ("In this sign you will conquer"). Emerging
from battle victorious, he became a Christian. It is a good
story, but that is not what "IHS" means. The letters "IHS"
are not Latin but Greek, the first three letters of the name
Jesus (I, *iota*; H, *'eta*; S, *sigma*) and are used as an abbreviation for that Holy Name. A cross with "IHS" on it is a less
obvious representation of Jesus crucified.

Orthodox crosses have two extra crosspieces, one above
and one below the main arms. The one above signifies the
placard nailed to the cross, proclaiming him "Jesus of Nazareth, King of the Jews" (in Latin: *Iesus Nazarenzus Rex
Iudiaorum*, INRI; see John 19:19). The lower crosspiece represents the foot piece to which were nailed the crucified person's feet. The crosspiece is at an angle, indicating the
suffering of Christ, who pressed down in pain, thus slanting
the footrest. In Orthodox churches Christ on the cross is usually represented in paintings with his feet nailed separately (in
Roman Catholic crucifixes, the feet are usually overlapped
and pierced with a single nail).

The cross, of course, is a scandal. That God should enter
human history in the person of Jesus Christ to be crucified is
nothing less than shocking. Yet in this ugly instrument of
death, God has worked the redemption of all the world and
conquered death. This paradox is preserved in the fact that
the cross has been glorified in jewelry and highly decorated
works of art, even by Protestants.

The following are the more commonly used crosses:

Latin Cross. This cross is shaped something like a lower
case "t" and, without the suffering body of Christ on it, is
said to represent the resurrection.

Greek (equal-armed) Cross. This cross's symmetry reflects the perfection of God's sacrificial love.

Tau Cross. Shaped like the Greek letter *tau* (a capital "T"), this is likely the style of cross actually used for the crucifixion, the crosspiece being carried by the victim and set atop the vertical part.

Orthodox Cross. Two additional crosspieces are on this cross, a shorter one above the main crosspiece representing the placard and another short one at an angle at the bottom of the cross representing the foot rest. The slanted crosspiece also may represent St. Andrew's cross, in that he was thought to have been the first missionary to Russia. This cross is used in Eastern churches.

Celtic Cross. A circle superimposed on the cross represents eternity or may be thought of as a nimbus or halo representing Christ. Ancient examples of this cross are found throughout Ireland and Scotland.

St. Andrew's Cross. According to tradition, Andrew was martyred by crucifixion, strapped to an X-shaped cross from which he preached before dying. The cross itself points to Christ, the X standing for chi, the first letter of Christ in Greek.

Jerusalem Cross. This cross is actually many crosses: four Tau crosses joined at their bases to form the main Greek cross and four smaller Greek crosses, one in each quadrant. These five crosses (the large cross and four smaller ones) may signify the five wounds of Christ (hands, feet, and side). The four Tau crosses may represent the spread of the gospel to the four corners or directions of the world. They or the four small crosses may suggest the four gospels presenting Christ.

(*See also* Cross, Sign of; Crucifixion; Symbols; X.)

Cross, Sign of.

The sign of the cross is a gesture employed in a variety of ways: a) toward others as a sign of blessing; b) on oneself from forehead to chest and shoulder to shoulder as a reminder of baptism; c) on one's own forehead; d) on another's forehead with oil as in anointing or the imposition of ashes.

The earliest form was probably on one's own forehead with the right thumb. Later it was traced from forehead to heart and then across the chest (left to right in Roman Catholic and Western churches, right to left in Eastern Orthodox churches). In many traditions, the sign of the cross is customarily made whenever the trinitarian formula is recited liturgically. The Orthodox place the thumb and first and second fingers together as a visual symbol of the Trinity as one crosses oneself.

Protestant Reformers rejected making the sign of the cross because they perceived it to be a kind of magical action as it was employed in the Middle Ages. They saw it used to guarantee the effectiveness of sacramental acts or simply to invoke divine intervention in daily events.

As a symbolic reminder of one's belonging to Christ, however, it may have usefulness in public worship as well as in personal piety. In the baptismal liturgy, for example, the sign of the cross is customary in anointing with oil the forehead of the baptized one. A broad sign of the cross may be traced by the minister over the congregation in the renewal of baptismal vows. It may also be done by a person as a reminder of one's own baptism. It is also sometimes employed as a visual affirmation of faith, a physical "Amen" interjected in worship at a particular point of significance for a given worshiper. Protestants are rediscovering the possibilities for this ancient gesture in modern circumstances. (*See also* Amen; Anointing; Ash Wednesday; Baptism; Cross; Crucifixion; Gesture and Posture; Renewal of Baptism.)

Crucifixion.

This was the common way to execute criminals in the time of Christ. A modern equivalent might be the electric chair. Crucifixion meant a most painful and dehumanizing death. Usually a person was stripped and exposed to the elements and the view of passersby. The person was fixed to a cross by nails through the hands and feet, lifted vertically, and left to hang. Hanging in that fashion, the person could not breathe because the lungs were constricted. By pressing against the nails in the feet, the person could get some air for a few moments until the pain in the feet became unbearable. Eventually the person would hang limp and suffocate. If death took too long, the attendants could hasten the process by breaking the person's legs to prevent the person from lifting up and breathing.

The danger today is the tendency to romanticize the death of Christ by making it sweet and even lovely. The crucifixion was an ugly and terrible thing; it should be remembered as such. The ugly and terrible deaths people die today may then be connected with Christ's death. This reference helps us try to prevent human suffering as we would try to prevent Christ's crucifixion. Also remembering the terror of Christ's death enables us to identify his suffering with ours in a redemptive way, confident that as Christ overcame death by death, so in our suffering and dying, Christ will bring us to new life. (*See also* Cross; Cross, Sign of; Good Friday; Resurrection.)

Daily Prayer.

Christian worship has never been limited to a once-a-week activity. While worship from the first celebrated Christ's resurrection on the Lord's Day, a simultaneous tradition of daily prayer has persisted. For the first Christians, daily prayer was part of their Jewish heritage. Morning and evening prayer times had long ago been established for the Jerusalem Temple, as well as for individuals, and became a style of prayer in the synagogues.

The early Christians perpetuated this pattern of morning and evening prayer, probably holding it in homes. The Psalter was also claimed by Christians as the center of daily prayer. While individual prayer was encouraged, corporate prayer was the norm. The mutual encouragement and discipline of the community were important in a Christian's prayer life.

When the period of persecution ended and Christianity became an established religion, daily prayer took two parallel
and often intertwining paths. One was the daily prayer of
congregations, which emphasized the participation of the
people in hymns and responses. The other was a monastic
style for clergy and those in orders, which developed more
complex music, set frequent times during the day for prayer,
and focused on praying through the Psalter on a regular
schedule. During the Middle Ages the latter form became
dominant.

The Protestant Reformation saw many attempts at reviv-
ing congregational daily prayer. Morning and evening prayer
were the norm; the language of the people was used rather
than Latin; Psalms and other biblical songs were arranged for
congregational singing, and the Bible was read straight
through a passage at a time, often with some sort of instruction. Daily prayer also found a focus in the family, who
would gather first thing in the morning and would also remain at the evening dinner table for scripture and prayer.
Daily prayer was also emphasized as a discipline for pastors:
the study became a chapel as scholarship and piety were
joined.

Daily prayer continues today as a vital aspect of Christian
worship. Christians have either gravitated toward the development of prayer books or have emphasized "free" prayer
(that is, prayer without set words or even structure but spon-
taneously offered) or have blended the two.

The prayer of the people each day is a reservoir for the
corporate prayers of the people on the Lord's Day. It is from
the daily discipline of the people that Lord's Day worship is
nourished and enriched so that the people participate in a
personal way. Corporate prayers of the gathered community
become personal as they are given content from the specific
daily prayers of the worshipers. The converse is also true,
however, in that Lord's Day worship gives experience and
examples of prayer for people to practice in their daily
disciplines.

While a separate two-year lectionary is often followed for

daily prayer, the Lord's Day three-year lectionary may easily be adapted for daily use. There are three lessons (Old Testament, New Testament Epistle, and Gospel) set for each Lord's Day for each of three years, for a total of nine readings per week. The three set for a Sunday may be reserved for that day, and the other six apportioned among the other six days of the week. Each passage may be read and reflected upon morning and evening. This practice reinforces appreciation of the lessons read on a given Sunday.

The basic structure of a daily prayer service is simple: psalmody, scripture, and prayer. The Psalms become our prayers and are shared in some participatory form, said or sung responsively or in metrical version. The scripture becomes the object of our meditation and prayerful reflection. The people engage in prayers that give voice to particular and even personal needs, shared in the community of faith. The prayers conclude with the Lord's Prayer. This pattern may be elaborated as appropriate for the circumstances of different groups.

While morning and evening are the basic times for daily prayer, some may want to set aside time in the middle of the day and before retiring at night. Prayer at midday is an extension of morning prayer, and night prayer continues evening prayer.

A discipline of daily prayer promises great benefits for a variety of groups of Christians, from committees, boards, and study groups in the local church, to regional and national governing bodies and conferences, from small groups of Christians in the work place to families gathered in homes. Each group will work out a style appropriate to its need. (*See also* Canticle; Lord's Prayer; Prayer; Psalter.)

Dance.

Physical movement is not alien to worship. Examples from the Bible indicate that dance has long had a religious function. The victorious crossing of the Red Sea by the people of Israel was celebrated in dance by Miriam (Exod. 15:20–21). David brought the Ark into the Holy City and "danced before the LORD with all his might" (2 Sam. 6:14) although this action did not meet with universal approval (see 2 Sam. 6:16). Even the prophetic vision of Jeremiah describes rejoicing in dance at the restoration of Israel (Jer. 31:4).

Even though dance was accepted in biblical times, the early church condemned it as degrading and unworthy of Christian participation because of its association with pagan and even Jewish worship. Philosophy and theology that saw the spiritual as good and eternal while the physical was evil and temporal did little to encourage any such display in worship. In the Middle Ages what dancing took place in churches was usually of a civic and social nature. Leaders of the Reformation were not supportive of the practice. Some Christians, however, did find something of value and, encouraged by biblical precedent, allowed, and in some cases affirmed, dance as a liturgical expression.

The Shakers are a prime example of advocates of dance. Most of their worship was centered around dance, hence their popular name. Believing that Christ was about to return, they considered dance the most appropriate expression of worship. Their arguments for dance in worship still have some validity. They affirmed the biblical precedent and saw dance as a gift of the Spirit to be employed, an activity to which humans are naturally disposed in rejoicing, which is appropriate to the Second Coming of Christ and our redemption, and which involves worshipers actively and corporately in the journey of faith.

A modern hymn has captured for us a sense of movement in worship. "I Danced in the Morning," written by Sydney Carter after an old English ballad, is appropriately set to a Shaker tune. It portrays the life of Christ as a dance in which disciples are invited to join. It describes the dance of life, a dance that sometimes is difficult but ultimately ends in rejoicing.

Dance in our worship is recognizable at least in the worshipers' entrance and departure. The prelude and postlude provide musical accompaniment to the gathering and scattering of the people of God.

Dance is also being rediscovered in churches as a medium for telling the gospel story, as an act of prayer, as a sign of celebration, as visual and physical interpretation of liturgical acts. Dance offers the possibility for the expression of the whole person in worship. As a corporate activity it can be a dynamic experience of unity in faith. (*See also* Carol; Procession; Recessional.)

Deacons.

The literal meaning of *deacon* is "one who serves or waits on tables." The title was given to servants of the church in the New Testament (see Acts 6:1–4, where the work of "serving" widows is assigned to seven people because the apostles did not consider it appropriate for them to give up the Word to "serve" or "wait on" tables; the word used here is the Greek word from which we get "deacon"). Apparently deacons soon began to serve the people the communion meal and most likely the agape or fellowship meals as well. It is easy to imagine that people would bring from home the bread and wine to be gathered by the deacons and shared at the Lord's Supper. The deacons would then take any surplus to the poor, infirm, or elderly. Soon people brought extra food not to be used at the sacrament but specifically to be given to the poor. Perhaps in this way the service of deacons at the Table became only a part of their larger service and ministry. Male and female deacons also assisted at baptisms.

In Reformed churches deacons are specifically charged with the ministry to the poor. Often a congregation will have a "deacons' fund" to provide for needs of the poor in the community. Deacons may work with civil agencies to meet human needs in feeding the hungry or housing the homeless. Through their ministry of service on behalf of the whole church, the deacons motivate other members to fulfill their responsibilities of Christian service.

It is significant that the service of deacons quickly found a place in the setting of worship, specifically at the Lord's Supper. In the Reformed tradition, deacons may still be called upon to assist in serving at the Lord's Table. It is the nature of Christian worship to point worshipers outward, so that worship is not merely an interior activity but the beginning of Christian service. Worship that does not send us out to serve, to practice what has been preached, to put prayers into action, is hardly worth the name.

The role of deacon varies in other traditions. The liturgical responsibilities of deacon are emphasized in the Roman Catholic Church and some others. Sometimes the office of deacon has been understood as a grade through which one passes on the way to priesthood. The Second Vatican Council made it a more permanent office, particularly in allowing married men to become deacons. Anglican and Methodist churches ordain women to this office. Orthodox churches also emphasize the liturgical role of deacons, with distinctive functions reserved for them alone. (*See also* Diakonia/Diaconate; Lord's Supper; Mission; Offering.)

Declaration of Faith.

See Confession of Faith.

Declaration of Forgiveness.

Following the confession of sin, there should be a declaration of God's mercy. Confession is not simply offered to convict a person of what is wrong, nor should its purpose be to inflict a burden of guilt. On the contrary, confession is a first step toward being freed of the dominion of sin and the weight of guilt. In Jesus Christ, God has offered liberation from sin's rule. In Jesus Christ, God has forgiven sin and healed the separation between God and humankind. This truth should be declared in clear, straightforward terms.

This statement of forgiveness is not a casual forgiveness of sins, moral infractions, or ethical failures but the essence of the gospel message. The abyss between God's righteousness and human disobedience is bridged in the life, death, and resurrection of Jesus Christ. It is in the declaration of forgiveness that the Good News of Jesus Christ is proclaimed, so that those who confess and repent may claim God's promised new life. What is more, this has already been accomplished by the grace of God and is not something we earn or deserve. The declaration of forgiveness reminds us that this is God's gift. (*See also* Confession of Sin; Good News.)

Decorations.

Decorations in the church enhance our worship by making the worship space attractive. Decorations should not be so lavish as to distract from the focus of worship.

Flowers are the usual decorations. Seasonal floral and other decorations from God's creation can enhance the worship of the Creator.

Other decorations may be of a more symbolic nature, employing the liturgical colors and symbols pertaining to the day or season of the Christian Year.

In the home decorations may be placed for the seasons of the Christian Year as a reminder of the worship of the gathered community on the Lord's Day. Those gathering at the family table or worship area for daily prayer will then have a sense of unity with the larger congregation of God's people. (*See also* Christian Year; Colors; Narthex; Symbols.)

Diakonia/Diaconate.

Diakonia is the Greek word for "service" and is used to describe the service of the church of Jesus Christ, who came not to be served but to serve. The diaconate refers to those called by the church to ensure that this particular ministry of service is fulfilled, namely deacons.

The church of Jesus Christ is always being sent out to serve its Servant Lord, and the only way to do this is to emulate the Master. When Jesus washed the feet of the disciples, he taught a lesson of service (see John 13:3–17).

Service of the church includes not merely almsgiving to poor, which can be condescending, but advocacy as well. The poor and disenfranchised are to be championed by the church.

Diakonia becomes a mandate for the church because in the experience of worship Christians encounter their Servant Lord. At the Table they receive Christ's self-giving; from the Table they go to give of themselves in Christ's name. (*See also* Deacons; Maundy Thursday; Mission.)

Discipline.

The word *discipline* comes from a Latin word meaning "instruction"; thus a disciple is one who learns. We come to worship to learn of God's will for us and our world. Worship, therefore, is a discipline. We do not come to worship to do as we please. We come in worship to do as God pleases, and we have seen God's pleasure in Jesus Christ, God's Word spoken in the flesh, God's Word revealed in scripture. There is always in worship a tension between freedom and formality. We tend to associate formality with rigidity and to put it in the same category as discipline. Freedom is far preferable, and that we associate with the Holy Spirit. Freedom, however, does not mean license to do what we please. Freedom implies its own discipline, for if we are free in Christ, we are bound to learn from him, to be his disciples, to follow closely in his steps. Our worship, therefore, is disciplined by the Word who calls us to be God's people, the Word who instructs us in scripture, the Word who feeds us at the Table, the Word who redeems us and the whole world. All we do in worship will be subject to the discipline of the Word in Jesus Christ and consistent with who Christ is.

It should be obvious that a part of discipline in worship is continued study, starting with study of the Word of God revealed in scripture. If we do not know who Jesus is, we may not recognize Christ as our risen Lord with us today. If we have not studied the scripture, we may not recognize the Word of God in sermon or sacrament in our worship. Discipline in study is an essential preparation for Christian worship.

Furthermore, if this is true for all worshipers, how much more important it is for leaders of worship—clergy, musicians, and others—to be in tune with scripture through disciplined study. The pastor particularly is the resident theologian. The people of the congregation should insist that their pastor engage in meaningful study of the Bible, as well as liturgy and theology, in a disciplined manner. (*See also* Bible/Scripture/Word of God; Lectionary; Preaching/Proclaiming the Word.)

Doxology.

Doxology literally means "words of glory." A doxology is, therefore, a glorification of God. Doxologies have been used by Jews and Christians as congregational responses and as the culmination of public prayer. They can take a variety of forms.

One traditional doxology is "Praise God, from Whom All Blessings Flow," usually set to the tune "Old Hundredth" from the Geneva Psalter of 1551. The words were written by Thomas Ken nearly a century and a half after the tune, but the two have been wedded in the minds and hearts of worshipers ever since. There are, however, other doxologies using Ken's words with new tunes, as well as different words set to the Old Hundredth tune.

Most anything can be called a doxology if it praises God. Usually doxologies take a trinitarian format, honoring God in three Persons, as Father, Son, and Holy Spirit. The Gloria Patri is a doxology, technically known as the "Lesser Doxology," although in many churches it is not called that so as to avoid confusion with the Thomas Ken text to "Old Hundredth." The Gloria Patri has been commonly appended to sung psalms and canticles, appropriating the biblical text for Christian worship. The "Greater Doxology" is the ancient hymn "Glory to God in the Highest," sung in Western churches at the Lord's Supper.

Often prayers will end with a doxological phrase, trinitarian in form, acknowledging that the prayer is to God, in the name of Jesus Christ, and by the power of the Holy Spirit. An expanded doxological ending is customary in the Great

Prayer of Thanksgiving of the Lord's Supper. Confessions of faith are sometimes concluded with a doxology. (*See also* Collect; Confession of Faith; Gloria Patri; Great Prayer of Thanksgiving.)

Drama.

Drama finds its roots in worship, albeit in pre-Christian Greek worship. The early church condemned such theatrical business, affirming that the only fit drama for Christians was that of the story of Christ enacted in the church. During the Middle Ages drama flourished in the church, as liturgy acted out the gospel. Morality plays sprouted from that seed, and theater further developed outside the church. With the Reformation came a renewed Christian condemnation of drama and theater, especially in Puritan England.

In modern times Christians have discovered that playwrights, whatever their religious perspective or lack thereof, have indeed dealt with the human drama and have portrayed the tragedy of sin's alienation as well as the triumph of redemption.

Christian worship is itself drama, portraying the story of Jesus Christ, in which we are all actors. There is a danger that worship may be thought of as dramatic in the sense of a performance to be viewed by the worshipers. It has been suggested that we can properly think of worship as drama, but we must get the assignments straight. Too often we think of God as the prompter; the preacher, choir, and worship leaders as the actors; and the congregation as the audience. The proper way to see worship as drama is to understand that God is the audience, the people are the performers, with the worship leaders as prompters.

This model for dramatic worship does several things:

1. The *people* are given their rightful role as actors in the drama of faith. The story of Christ sooner or later must become our story, or else it is a long-ago-and-far-away tale that has little or nothing to do with us today.

2. The *preacher* is delivered from giving a performance but

is compelled to exhort the people as directed by the "script," the scripture. This keeps the preacher accountable to the story. The preacher is a prompter, not a performer. As a prompter the preacher has a vested interest in the "performance" of the people, that their praise and resulting witness and service will be "according to the scriptures."

3. The *choir and other musicians* are similarly called to sing and play on behalf of the congregation, not as a substitute for but for the encouragement of the congregation's praise of God. Applause by the congregation for an anthem of the choir, for instance, is inappropriate, for it immediately shifts all the roles around, giving praise to people rather than to God.

God is the audience, the One who hears our praise, the One who receives our worship. All we say and do in worship is directed toward God. Our reason for being there is to praise God for all God has done for us, as we remember it in our history and as it is recorded in the pages of scripture. The content of our worship is the drama played out between God and the people of God in the Bible, a drama that continues to be acted out each Lord's Day when we come to worship.

Drama, therefore, is appropriate in the setting of Lord's Day worship when it displays the drama of God's mighty acts. The enactment or choral reading of a scripture lesson, for instance, will dramatize the gospel, not as a performance for the congregation, but as a way of including the congregation in the biblical story. Drama as an act of worship can involve each person as a participant on the stage of faith with Jesus Christ. In this way one demonstrates and enacts one's struggle with faith as well as one's acknowledgment of grace before the supreme audience, God. (*See also* Anthem; Bible/Scripture/Word of God; Choir; Congregation; Preaching/Proclaiming the Word.)

Easter.

The name *Easter* is said to have been adapted from a goddess whose festival was celebrated at the vernal equinox, the time of year when the duration of daylight equals and begins to surpass that of darkness. Easter is related to the Jewish Passover and its date is determined by a lunar calendar as is that of Passover. For Western Christians Easter is the first Sunday after the full moon on or after March 21 and can fall any time from March 22 to April 25. Orthodox churches follow a different calendar in their calculations, and their Easter rarely falls on the same date as in the West.

Easter began as an observance of the death and resurrection of Christ. By the fourth century, however, Good Friday became the observance of the crucifixion, and Easter was left to emphasize the resurrection.

The Lord's Supper is rightly celebrated on Easter Day although the tone places more emphasis on the resurrection meals rather than on the Last Supper. The triumph of Jesus Christ over death is the joyful theme.

Easter is also a season of fifty days (sometimes called "The Great Fifty Days") running from Easter Sunday to Pentecost (from the Greek for "fifty"). This seven-week period was observed early in the church's history, giving an opportunity to explore the depth of meaning in the resurrection event. Easter is the great validation of Jesus Christ and deserves a full celebration. It is the longest season of the Christian year for this reason.

Furthermore, Easter is the model for every Sunday. Worship on the Lord's Day is always a celebration of the resurrection as the victory of Jesus Christ over death and the deliverance of God's people from sin's dominion. (*See also* Christian Year; Easter Vigil; Good Friday; Lord's Day/Sunday/Sabbath; Lord's Supper; Resurrection; Season.)

Easter Vigil.

According to the ancient way of reckoning, the day began with sundown, a pattern recorded in Genesis and one that has continued in Jewish observance. Chaos of night gives way to the order of the day in the Genesis creation, and, in

Christ's story, the darkness of death is followed by the dawn of resurrection in the new creation.

Easter, therefore, begins in the dark as the congregation gathers to light a fire, symbolic of Christ, from which is lit a candle to lead them in procession as they sing. After singing God's praise in the Exsultet, the story of God's redemptive acts is rehearsed from scripture, beginning with creation, the rescue of Noah, the call of Abraham, the deliverance of Israel from bondage, on through the cry of the prophets, culminating with the crucifixion and resurrection of Jesus Christ. Throughout this rehearsal of salvation history, candles may be lighted and the room slowly brightened, looking toward the dawning of Easter Day. It is a "vigil" because it is a time of waiting for God once again to come for our redemption. It is a time of anticipating the Easter joy by remembering the wonders of God's grace and God's love for all people.

The Easter Vigil (often called the Paschal Vigil, see below) is one of the oldest liturgical observances of the Christian church. From the very beginning, followers of the risen Christ rehearsed his story, not simply to remember him, but to recognize his saving presence. This marvelously rich service is being reclaimed in many Protestant churches, as it has been continued in Roman Catholic and Orthodox traditions, fully displaying the Good News of Jesus Christ in readings, prayers, and sacraments. It is a fitting climax to Lent, providing an opportunity for recommitment at the end of a season of personal reflection and renewal.

It is appropriate at the Easter Vigil to include the sacrament of baptism or at least the renewal of baptismal vows since Lent originated as a time of preparing candidates for their baptisms. Baptism can be celebrated in the service at a point between the Old Testament readings and those of the New Testament, when the mood shifts to bright resurrection themes. The Lord's Supper is celebrated as well, recalling resurrection meals and the Messianic Banquet at the end of time as well as the Last Supper. The Christian Passover (sometimes called *Pasch* or *Pascha*, from the Hebrew word for "deliver-

ance" or "passover") rehearses the deliverance of God's people in the death and resurrection of Jesus Christ. (*See also*
Baptism; Candles; Easter; Exsultet; Lent; Lord's Supper; Pascha; Paschal Candle; Procession; Salvation History.)

Ecstatic Utterances/Speaking in Tongues.

The practice of ecstatic utterances in worship stems from
the entrance of the Gentiles into the Christian community
(see Acts 10–11). It was a part of non-Jewish worship to display enthusiasm openly, and Gentile converts did just that in
Christian worship to the point that it became a problem. Paul
wrote to the Corinthian Christians advising them to do all
things "decently and in order" (1 Cor. 14:40).

"Speaking in tongues" (the technical term is "glossolalia,"
which means simply that) is a different matter, stemming as it
does from the experience of the apostles at Pentecost (Acts 2).
Here, inspired by God's Spirit, the apostles spoke in languages of the world that were understood by those who had
come from many different countries to Jerusalem for the festival. Speaking in tongues is not nonsensical babbling but
communicating the gospel message. It is not for the benefit of
the speaker but for the hearer. Paul does not forbid speaking
in tongues but insists it be done in orderly fashion and in a
nondisruptive way. His counsel is that speaking in tongues
requires interpretation (1 Cor. 14:27–28), and if there is no
interpretation, then there should be no speaking in tongues.

Many Christians have approached ecstatic utterances and
speaking in tongues with caution, for while these actions are
among the spiritual gifts, they are clearly low on the list
(compare the list of spiritual gifts in 1 Cor. 12:4–11 with that
in Rom. 12:6–8). All too often ecstatic utterances have the
effect of being divisive rather than unifying as they should be.
The test is always whether the ecstatic utterance contributes
to the unity of the church and the edification of the hearers.

In spite of all this caution, there is a sense in which abandon is appropriate to worship as one surrenders oneself to

God. Certainly enthusiasm is to be welcomed and encouraged in worship, in the fervency of prayer, the vitality of
preaching, and the zest of singing God's praise. (*See also*
Charism/Charisma/Charismatic.)

Ecumenism.

Ecumenism refers to the global nature of the church of
Jesus Christ. We need to remember that we are not ourselves
the whole church, much less the true church. Yet when we
worship on the Lord's Day, we are representative of the
whole church. Each congregation is a microcosm of the
whole body of Christ.

What we learn ecumenically, that is from other Christian
traditions and experiences, is important to the fullness of our
worship. Not all practices of other Christians will be appropriate for the use of every congregation. But other Christians'
practices in worship can be respected and understood in order
to learn from them.

Roman Catholics can teach something of the drama of the
liturgy, for example, and the Orthodox can educate about the
power of image and color. Pentecostals can prompt the freedom of faith's expression, while Methodists can instruct in
disciplined worship. Each tradition has something unique to
offer all the others. It is in giving and receiving among traditions that all gain some notion of the fullness of the Christian
faith and the richness of God's gifts to the whole church. (*See
also* Koinonia; Lectionary.)

Elders.

The term "elder" translates a Greek word, *presbyteros*,
which refers literally to an older person. A synonym, therefore, for "elder" is "presbyter." The word was used in biblical
times by Jews and Christians to denote both older people in
general and people who were designated to positions of responsibility and authority if not simply because of their age,
then because of the wisdom that comes with age.

Modern usage may or may not have much to do with age but does emphasize responsibility and authority. Elders in the Reformed tradition are elected by the congregation to govern it. A major responsibility of elders (who collectively make up the governing board of a local church) is that of worship. Elders have responsibilities to provide for preaching, the sacraments, corporate prayer, and music, and a wide-ranging authority to oversee and approve all public worship of the local church.

While there is a separation of powers between the elders and the minister in a local church (the elders in governing and the minister in preaching the Word and administering the sacraments), governance covers worship, too. The minister is to assist the people in *their* worship, and the representatives of the people, the elders, by their oversight ensure ownership of congregational worship by the people.

In some parts of the Reformed tradition it has been the custom to refer to the minister as a "teaching elder" to distinguish her or him from the "ruling elder" who governs. The teaching role of the minister is certainly important and is related to the minister's responsibility for preaching. This term also suggests that the minister shares with elders in the ministry of governance. (*See also* Minister; Service for the Lord's Day; Vestments/Robes/Stoles.)

Entrance.

See Procession.

Epiclesis.

This Greek word is usually translated as "invocation." It refers specifically to that part of the Great Prayer of Thanksgiving at the Lord's Supper that asks God to send the Holy Spirit so that sharing in the bread and wine may be communion in the body and blood of Christ. A similar prayer is offered over the water at baptism, invoking the Spirit's empowerment of the sacrament.

The epiclesis is a reminder that the sacraments are not human actions but God's actions. It is only by the grace of God and the power of the Holy Spirit that the Lord's Supper is communion with God and that baptism is dying and rising with Christ into new life. We do not celebrate these sacraments to manipulate God to do what we want. Rather, the sacraments are to acknowledge God's saving power, claim God's promises of new life, and commit ourselves anew to do what God wants. (*See also* Baptism; Great Prayer of Thanksgiving; Holy Spirit; Invocation; Lord's Supper.)

Epiphany.

Epiphany Day, January 6, may be thought of as the end of the Christmas season. *Epiphany* is from a Greek word meaning "manifestation" or "showing forth." The day gathers a number of traditional themes: the birth of Jesus as God's incarnation, the coming of the Magi, Christ's baptism in the Jordan, and Jesus' first miracle at the wedding at Cana. All of these "manifest" Jesus as being the Christ, God-with-us, the Light of the world.

The color for Epiphany is white, representing the brightness of Christ shining for the world to see. Gold may also be used. (*See also* Baptism of the Lord; Christian Year; Christmas.)

Epistle.

The word *epistle* is from the Greek word meaning "letter" and is usually applied to one of the New Testament letters. In a service of worship, the Epistle is the second reading of a set of three, the first from the Old Testament (Hebrew Scriptures) and the third from one of the Gospels. Sometimes the epistle lesson is not from a letter at all but may be from Acts or Revelation. Therefore the term may apply to the New Testament reading that is not the Gospel.

The New Testament epistles were written to real people in Christian congregations and deserve to be heard today as similarly addressed. They provide for us a sense of continuity with the church through the ages. The spiritual struggles recorded there are common today and the encouragements and instructions seem strangely relevant.

The preacher may want to follow (as lectionaries often do) passages of an epistle in sequence to explore in a series of sermons the themes of the letter. Since the epistles were originally written to be read in print, they lend themselves to study and reflection. Brief passages lifted out of context are for this reason sometimes difficult to comprehend. (*See also* Bible/Scripture/Word of God; Lectionary; Preaching/Proclaiming the Word; Service for the Lord's Day.)

Eucharist.

See Lord's Supper.

Eucharistic Prayer.

See Great Prayer of Thanksgiving.

Exsultet (Exultet).

The *Exsultet* (also spelled *Exultet*) is a song of praise sung by cantor and congregation at the Easter Vigil, following the procession of the Paschal candle and before the readings of scripture: "Rejoice, heavenly powers! Sing, choirs of angels! Jesus Christ our King is risen!" This Easter proclamation dates from the seventh century. It calls the church and the whole creation to exult because of Christ's victory over death and darkness. It continues as a sung prayer, rejoicing in the wondrous mercy of God's redemption in Jesus Christ, likening the Easter deliverance to the Exodus. It concludes by offering the Paschal candle as an evening sacrifice. (*See also* Easter Vigil; Paschal Candle.)

Fasting.

See Lent.

Father, Son, and Holy Spirit.

The "Trinitarian Formula" is more than just a rote phrase. It provides us with an important insight into God's nature.

"Father," "Son," and "Holy Spirit" are the names of the "persons" of the Trinity. God is not an abstraction but is to be known personally.

We know this God by name. Jesus called God "Father" and "Abba," an Aramaic word infants used to address a parent (such as "Mama" or "Daddy" today), often the first word a child learned, a name for the first person a child recognized. There is an essential intimacy to the relationship between God and the people, one that suggests the bond of love and ultimate trust.

We also know this God through Jesus Christ, the "Son" of God who belongs to God in a particular way. Surely, all people may be broadly understood as children of God. Yet Christ is God's Son in a unique way, for Jesus is the one who incorporates both deity and humanity.

Holy Spirit is also a description of God. Sometimes God is experienced as a power beyond our own, or as peace deep within, or even as unity that binds us to one another. This we call Holy Spirit. "Spirit" translates Hebrew and Greek words for "wind" and "breath." God is sometimes like the wind, impossible to see, but apparent in activity and force. God is sometimes the life-giving breath in each of us, that close, that necessary.

The three persons of the Trinity are not three different gods, independent of one another. Rather they are intimately interrelated in one unity.

This traditional formula has caused some consternation in recent years in that it relies heavily on masculine imagery in the descriptions of God as Father and Son. Some have suggested alternative phrases, the most popular of which is "Creator, Redeemer, Sustainer." There are three basic problems with this substitute. One is that it does not acknowledge that Jesus himself taught us to address God as "Father" and that Jesus was himself a man. While the first term is metaphor, the second is simply a statement of fact. Another problem with any substitute is that it does not take into account ecumenical practice. To abandon the traditional formula is to reject centuries of common usage by Christians around the world.

This cannot be done lightly. A final problem is that the terms "Creator, Redeemer, and Sustainer" are not really titles or names, but refer to functions of the Deity and might justifiably be assigned to all three persons of the Trinity. Jesus Christ was a participant in creation (John 1:1–4), as was the Spirit (Gen. 1:2), so "Creator" is inaccurate if applied to the first person of the Trinity alone. Similarly, God "the Father" and the Spirit participate in the redemptive act, while Jesus Christ and God "the Father" are also involved in sustaining the children of God.

While there is yet to be a satisfactory solution, the ecumenical agenda in the generations to come will continue to include discussion of the problem of masculine dominance of traditional imagery regarding God. The Trinitarian Formula may find new expression in the fullness of time. (*See also* God; Holy Spirit; Jesus Christ; Language of Worship.)

Font, Baptismal.

The word *font* is derived from a Latin word meaning "spring of water," from which our word "fountain" also comes. The term is applied to a piece of furniture found in Christian churches and used at the sacrament of baptism. The shape and location of the font can say a great deal about the meaning of the sacrament for that particular church.

While most fonts are mere receptacles to hold water for baptism, the term itself suggests running water (sometimes called "living" water). The implication is that baptismal water is life-giving, as the one baptized is brought to new life in Jesus Christ. The font may also be in the form of a pool, into which one descends to be baptized, to rise again to new life in Jesus Christ.

Baptismal fonts are often octagonal, eight-sided, because the number eight is associated with the resurrection. Jesus was raised from the dead on the eighth day after entering Jerusalem; creation took place in seven days, the new creation in the resurrection on the eighth; and early Christians thought of Noah's ark with its eight passengers as typifying baptism, as they were delivered by water to start human history again. The number eight is also associated with baptism because it replaced circumcision as the sign of the covenantal relationship between God and the people of God. Jewish boy babies were circumcised traditionally on the eighth day after their birth, and baptism was hence sometimes considered the "Christian circumcision."

Roman Catholics and some other Christians remember their baptisms by placing small fonts inside the entrances of their churches. As people enter, they touch some of the water to their foreheads as a reminder that it is by baptism that they became part of the church. As they exit, they do the same thing, reminding themselves to live out their baptisms with the risen Christ.

In some Protestant churches, the font is placed centrally so it may be obvious to the worshipers as a reminder of their baptisms. Occasionally the font is placed at the church entrance as a visual reminder of entering the church by baptism and leaving worship to go into the world as baptized disciples of Jesus Christ. Even when not in use, the font may occupy a prominent place. To move the font to another place when not in use discounts its symbolic significance. If the font is positioned at one side, it may suggest that baptisms are private rather than congregational acts. (*See also* Baptism; Renewal of Baptism.)

Footwashing.

See Maundy Thursday.

Funeral.

From the very beginning, the Christian church has acted out its faith in the face of death. What we know today as the funeral service has a long and complex history, with its roots in the practices of the early church, which included prayers in the home (where death usually occurred) as the body was prepared, a service of prayer and praise with the Lord's Supper, and burial.

These essential ingredients are found in Christian ceremonies today. Pastoral visits with the family at the time of
death or shortly thereafter usually include prayers of praise
and thanksgiving for the life of the deceased as well as concern for the family. The service at the church may include
the placing of the pall and procession of the casket, a
prayer of confession and declaration of pardon, readings
from scripture and a sermon, a confession of faith, prayers,
the Lord's Supper, the commendation, and dismissal. The
commendation is essentially a prayer entrusting the
deceased person to God's eternal care and is a helpful conclusion to the service in the church since many people at-
tending may not go to the graveside. The committal is the
service at the graveside, which may be held before the
church service so that the family may stay after the church
service to be greeted by friends.

The Christian funeral is a witness to the resurrection, a
time to confront the mystery of death with an affirmation of
faith. Whether the service is technically a funeral service
(with the body present) or a memorial service (held some time
after the burial), the content is the same. Rejoicing in the resurrection of Jesus Christ, Christians affirm that those who
live and die in Christ all share in that resurrection.

It is important to distinguish between "the immortality of
the soul," on the one hand, and "the resurrection of the
body," on the other. The former is a Greek concept that suggests that while the part of a person we call the soul lives on
after the death of the body, the body is basically a prison for
the soul. Death liberates the soul. Thus people do not really
die but live in a different nonphysical state. The biblical understanding of the "resurrection of the body," however, indicates that the whole person dies at death and that Almighty
God raises the dead to life, just as God raised Jesus from the
dead. The death of Jesus was real, total, and complete; so is
the death of anyone else. Christians accept the reality of
death and affirm their sure and certain hope of the resurrection of the whole person, body and soul.

Funeral practices and liturgies should be examined with

care for confusions between these two views. Often funeral practices dictated by custom will announce the unreality of death and make healthy grieving difficult. If the liturgy glosses over human mortality, then those who worship at a funeral will not face the reality of death and will be distracted from considering their own needs before God. Stressing immortality tends to obscure the gospel of Jesus Christ, which affirms that we are all mortals and our time on earth is fleeting, and that Christ has shared in our mortality so that we might in God's mercy know a new life with him.

When a funeral or memorial service is to be planned, the family of the deceased and the pastor should work together. The pastor provides resources for the family members to enable them to worship as fully as possible. There are many standard liturgical resources, familiar passages of scripture, and favorite hymns from which the family may select what is most meaningful. Celebration of the Lord's Supper should also be considered as part of this planning. Other liturgical opportunities may be considered as well that enable the family to engage most significantly in worship of God, such as placing a pall on the casket at the beginning of the service and the renewal of baptismal vows.

Funeral services have this in common with worship on the Lord's Day: both celebrate the resurrection of Jesus Christ. It is appropriate, therefore, not only when a funeral takes place on a Sunday, but even when it does not, that some elements of a church member's funeral be included in Lord's Day worship. Certainly the person's death should be announced. The congregation might be invited to pray in silence or during the intercessions, giving thanks for the life of the deceased and offering prayers for the comfort of the bereaved.

It is helpful for the governing body of a particular church to establish policies about funerals, including the desirability of holding funerals in the church, the use of a pall to cover the casket, appropriate music, and other matters. (*See also* Lord's Day/Sunday/Sabbath; Lord's Supper; Ordinances; Pall; Pastoral Care; Procession; Resurrection; Service for the Lord's Day; Worship Committee.)

Gathering.

See Call to Worship; Congregation; Prelude; Procession; Service for the Lord's Day.

Gesture and Posture.

A gesture may be understood as a movement or placement of one's hands, arms, head, legs, or body as an act of worship. Posture is a stationary physical position that has significance in worship. Among Christians there are several gestures and postures employed regularly in worship. Some have long traditions associated with them, and many are traced to biblical sources.

Protestant Christians have generally felt uncomfortable with gestures in worship although attitudes have changed in recent years. The discomfort comes from several directions. For one thing, Protestants have understood themselves in part, at least, as being in opposition to Roman Catholics. Gestures long employed by Roman Catholics have been rejected by many Protestants simply for that reason. The Reformers did not reject the gestures themselves but the superstitions that accompanied them. Any idea that one could manipulate God by an appropriate liturgical gesture was offensive. Protestant worship has also tended to be more austere than Orthodox and Roman Catholic. Gestures have been kept to a minimum as have other visual symbols.

Furthermore, Protestant worshipers have assumed a basically passive role in worship rather than an active one. The people in the pew can more easily accept a gesture on the part of the clergy worship leader than for themselves since they are watching rather than performing.

The main gesture used by a Protestant worshiper is *bowing the head* (and closing the eyes) for prayer. The bowed head shows humility in approaching God and also enables prayer to be intimate and personal. It risks making prayer an individual activity rather than a communal one.

Standing is a common posture. Standing for hymns, in particular, is appropriate for the praise of God. The reason why worshipers stand to sing may sometimes be more practical than symbolic: one sings better when standing. Those who plan worship should resist the temptation, however, to place a hymn in the order only so that pew-sitters can stretch their legs. Standing up as a gesture and the posture of standing should be employed meaningfully.

Standing is primarily a posture for praise and is appropriate not only for singing hymns but also for creedal affirmations and prayers of praise, particularly the Great Prayer of Thanksgiving in the Lord's Supper.

Standing also communicates a sense of honor and respect as well as attention and readiness to act. It is the custom in many churches for all to stand for the reading of the Gospel lesson. The Gospel proclaims Christ who confronts the listeners with a call to discipleship; standing indicates the respect and eagerness of the hearers to do what Christ bids.

Standing for prayer is also common and has biblical precedent to recommend it (see 1 Sam. 1:26 and 1 Kings 8:22). It was common in the time of Jesus as well (note Matt. 6:5 and Luke 18:11), but kneeling was also practiced among early Christians (see Luke 22:41 and Acts 7:60).

In worship bulletins and in spoken liturgical instructions, care should be exercised to be sensitive to those with physical handicaps. "Let us all stand" may not be an appropriate instruction if there are worshipers present confined to wheelchairs. "Let those who are able stand for the reading of the Gospel" is better but still calls attention to the disabilities of the few. People who are handicapped in this way should be consulted about the most helpful ways of expressing such instructions.

Sitting is the most common posture in Christian worship although this is not universally true. Pews, chairs or benches are relatively modern furnishings for Christian churches. In the early centuries, as in many European churches today, places to sit were not available except for the bishop and elders. (The one who presided at worship was called *president*, literally, "one who sits before.") Seats for others, placed around pillars or walls of the building, were first provided for the disabled and infirm.

The posture of sitting is appropriate for receiving instruction, hearing the scripture and sermon. It is often considered an alternative to kneeling as a posture for prayer.

Kneeling is also a common posture. Kneeling for prayer suggests humility before God, placing oneself under God's direction. In ancient times, kneeling was the posture for penitents, not for all, at the beginning of the service. Some churches provide kneeling benches or cushions in the pews and may have special pieces of furniture for brides and grooms to use for a wedding prayer.

Kneeling is also the posture for ordination, installation, and confirmation, in each case suggesting a willingness of the person to be subject to God's will.

The *laying on of hands* is a multifaceted gesture signifying the bestowing of God's grace. It is employed at ordination, baptism, confirmation, and in situations of pastoral care, such as prayers with the sick.

The *folding of hands* or placing the hands palms together in prayer is a stereotypical gesture. It signifies petition, asking for something, even pleading.

The *sign of the cross* is used most commonly by Orthodox, Anglican, and Roman Catholic Christians, as well as some others. Worshipers make the sign on themselves either broadly from forehead to chest and shoulder to shoulder or in a small form on the forehead. The sign of the cross may also be made by the clergy or worship leaders with the right hand as a blessing in the direction of others. Clergy may use it on another's forehead in anointing or marking with ashes. The gesture is also used to bless communion elements and offerings. Many Protestants today are reviewing the appropriate use of the sign of the cross as a helpful symbolic gesture for worship.

Blessings are ordinarily given by the *raising of one or both hands*, palms down, over the people as they bow their heads, indicating their humble acceptance of God's blessings. The benediction of a service is usually given in this way.

Hands raised, palms up, often indicate reaching up toward God, a spatial symbol used metaphorically. The custom of

lifting the hands for prayer has biblical foundations
(Ps. 141:2) and is employed in this sense.

Folding the arms across one's chest is also a gesture referring to prayer. An Orthodox Christian making the sign of the
cross will wind up with the arm across the breasts, initiating a
posture of prayer. Pretzels (sometimes called "prayer bread")
are associated with prayer for this reason. The word *pretzel* is
related to our word "brace," referring to the two arms folded
in prayer.

Genuflecting, the act of touching the knee to the floor, is a
sign of reverence. While originally being a simple enactment
of the biblical statement that "at the name of Jesus every
knee should bend" (Phil. 2:10), it came to be a sign of reverence toward the elements of the sacrament and was rejected
as such by the Reformers.

The kiss of peace, or the greeting of peace, is an ancient
gesture reclaimed in the twentieth century for broad use. It
may take the form of a kiss, an embrace, or a handclasp, and
all three options are often offered to worshipers. It is a powerful symbol, allowing physical expression of the unity worshipers have with one another in Jesus Christ. As a reminder
of Judas' kiss of betrayal, it calls worshipers to sober reflection. (*See also* Baptism; Blessing; Bulletin; Confirmation;
Cross, Sign of; Great Prayer of Thanksgiving; Hymn; Laying
on of Hands; Ordination; Pastoral Care; Pew; Prayer; Service
for Wholeness.)

Gloria Patri.

Gloria Patri is Latin for "Glory Be to the Father," the first
line of a trinitarian song of praise sometimes called "the
Lesser Doxology." There is a long tradition of using the Gloria Patri after singing psalms, perhaps as a way of "christian-
izing" the psalms for Christian worship.

In modern times the Gloria Patri has been commonly
sung set to a tune composed in 1851 by Henry W.
Greatorex, an English musician who served a variety of
churches in America, or chanted to an old Scottish chant of

unknown origin. Other musical settings are appropriate as well.

The text was formulated as early as the second century to emphasize the Trinity, following the trinitarian formula given by Christ in the Great Commission (Matt. 28:19). (*See also* Chant; Doxology.)

God.

God is the One who makes worship possible. Without the mighty acts of God creating and redeeming the world in Jesus Christ by the power of the Holy Spirit, we would be without cause for praise. We worship because of who God is and what God has done, and because of what we expect God to do.

Usually in our worship we address God as God, but that is not God's name. God's name was revealed to Moses in Exodus when the voice from the burning bush answered Moses' request for a name with the cryptic "I Am Who I Am." The Hebrew characters of that name transliterate as *YHWH*, sometimes spelled out as "Yahweh" or "Jehovah."

Jesus taught his followers to call God "Father." There are many other names and descriptions of God found in the Bible as well, and they deserve to be used as we remember that God's greatness cannot be captured by any one name or description.

God is both transcendent and immanent, wholly other and therefore holy, and at the same time merciful and intimate. God confronts us with the mystery of the incarnation: how could God, Creator of the universe, become a mere mortal, and why would God do that? While incarnation is probably impossible to explain, it is certainly our experience that this is exactly what God has done in Jesus Christ. God has come to be one of us, one with us, in the human being Jesus of Nazareth. God translated into human form is Jesus. In living the human life of Jesus, God has redeemed all human life and restored to everyone the possibility of living a new life as God originally intended, the life we have failed to live. If Adam and Eve are models of sinful life, lives that have

fallen short of being what God wants, then Jesus is our model
for redeemed life, life with God, what God intends for each
of us, eternal life. It is by the power of God's Spirit that we
recognize God in Jesus Christ and are enabled to follow
Christ.

When we celebrate the incarnation, our worship of God
becomes intensely personal. That is not to say worship is individual, for God has called us out to be a people, not merely
a group of individuals. Even as a people, we are personally
related to God, and our worship deals with life-and-death
issues.

A problem persists at this point. How can we speak of such
a God, one who is both utterly other and intimately personal?
If God were only transcendent, we could think of and speak
of God in impersonal terms. In that instance, we would probably have little occasion to address God at all. God, however,
is both transcendent and immanent, both beyond our comprehension and personal. So we are called to speak with God,
to engage in the conversation of prayer, and to share with
others what we know about God.

At this point our language fails us. English-speaking people, in particular, are limited by the personal pronouns available, either masculine or feminine. Yet God is neither
masculine or feminine. If we do not refer to God as "he" or
"she," what are our alternatives? The use of the neutral pro-
noun, "it," is unsatisfactory since it destroys any personal
quality. God would become a thing rather than a person.
Some have employed the artifice of alternating "he" and
"she," which I find distracting and, in the long run, inadequate. Another alternative is to refer to God without using
personal pronouns at all, by using God, the Almighty, or the
Deity. If not done carefully, this can be cumbersome. It does
not solve the problem of reflexive pronouns. For example, it
is common to refer to God as revealing "himself." One may
say "God's Self," or that God is self-revealing, but this loses
both the power and the personal quality of the revelation.

The problem is essentially that all human language is inadequate to speak of God. At best all our words about God are

metaphor, and all our liturgical language is poetry. God being God, and we being who we are, we find it impossible to formulate adequate words to describe God. Still we should not let the limitations of our language limit our understanding of God. We may address God as "Father" or "Mother," but we do so fully aware that God is not simply like human parents, nor is God like humans at all. We do not fashion God in our image. On the contrary, we are fashioned in God's own image, whether we are male or female of whatever race or color. God is far greater than any human differences or distinctions.

Because God is Ruler of the universe, all of life is fit to be brought into worship and held up before God. Because God is our Redeemer in Jesus Christ, the most personal aspects of all our lives may be part of our worship. Worship is a point of encounter between God and the people of God, between the Ruler of all time and space and each of us. Here, in our worship, the abyss of sin is bridged because Christ has once and for all reconnected us sinners with the Holy One. In our worship, God's promises of renewal, healing, and restoration are kept, and we come to praise God with hearts overflowing because of God's grace and love. In our worship, God's Spirit draws us close to God in Jesus Christ and close to one another in the community of the church. (*See also* Father, Son, and Holy Spirit; Language of Worship.)

Godparents.

See Sponsors.

Going forth.

See Mission; Recessional; Service for the Lord's Day.

Good Friday.

Why is this day called "good"? The term emphasizes that God takes what is utterly evil and claims it for good purposes. The crucifixion of Jesus was not a good thing, not by any stretch of the imagination, but God wrestled with this monstrous evil committed by humans and won a victory out of it. The very death of Christ became the salvation of humankind. By death, Jesus conquered death itself for all of us. This fact is often celebrated in the "Memorial Acclamation."

Good Friday is traditionally observed by worship that remembers the seven last words of Christ from the cross:

"Father, forgive them; for they do not know what they are doing" (Luke 23:34).

"Today you will be with me in Paradise" (Luke 23:43).

"Woman, here is your son. . . . Here is your mother" (John 19:26–27).

"My God, my God, why have you forsaken me?" (Matt. 27:46; Mark 15:34; see also Ps. 22:1).

"I am thirsty" (John 19:28).

"It is finished" (John 19:30).

"Father, into your hands I commend my spirit" (Luke 23:46; see also Ps. 31:5).

The Tenebrae (from the Latin for "shadows") service has been related to the observance of Good Friday from the Middle Ages, as candles are snuffed throughout the reading of the story of Jesus' Passion. Today this service is often included in Maundy Thursday evening observances.

Good Friday appears in the midst of the "Great Three Days" or the *Triduum* (Latin for "Three Days"), flanked by Maundy Thursday and Holy Saturday with the Easter Vigil. These days are of a piece, as the Passion story is acted out by the rehearsal of the Last Supper, the crucifixion, and the day of silence before the triumph of Easter.

It is appropriate that no liturgical colors or other decorations be used on this day. The worship space may be stripped bare at the end of the Maundy Thursday service in preparation for Good Friday. If color is to be used, it may be either purple (as for the rest of Lent), black (the color of mourning), or dark red (to symbolize the blood of Christ). (*See also* Acclamation; Crucifixion; Easter Vigil; Holy Saturday; Holy Week; Maundy Thursday; Procession; Solemn Reproaches from the Cross; Tenebrae; Triduum.)

Good News.

Good News refers specifically to the message of God's love for all humankind seen in Jesus Christ. It is a literal translation of a Greek word from which we get our word "evangelism." The word "gospel" comes from an older English word meaning "Good News." (*See also* Gospel.)

Gospel.

Gospel is a modern corruption of an Anglo-Saxon word "Godspell," translating a Greek word that means literally, "Good News." There is, however, a happy ambiguity in the term, for "Godspell" also translates as "God's story." Putting the two together, we discover that gospel indicates the good news of love in God's story throughout all times.

Specifically, the term refers to each of the first four books collected in the New Testament: Matthew, Mark, Luke, and John. The first three are known as "Synoptic" Gospels because they "see together," agreeing in many details about the story of Jesus Christ they record.

The Gospel reading in worship is the culmination of the series of scripture readings. In the Gospel the Word, Jesus Christ, is supremely presented. The Word is heard in the other readings as well, but the Gospels were explicitly written to proclaim Jesus Christ. This reading in worship has special significance, signaled by its place at the end of the readings and usually immediately preceding the sermon. The Gospel should always be read when the Lord's Supper is celebrated so that the connection between the Word proclaimed in scripture and the Word enacted in sacrament is clearly made.

It is customary in many traditions for people to stand to hear the Gospel lesson. This is a symbolic gesture signifying the honoring of the Gospel by the people and also the intent of the people to be on their feet, ready to obey the Gospel commands. In some traditions incense is burned to honor the Gospel, and often a candle is lighted or placed near the lectern as the Gospel is read to represent the light of Jesus Christ shining through the text. (*See also* Bible/Scripture/Word of

God; Gesture and Posture; Incense; Preaching/Proclaiming the Word.)

Great Prayer of Thanksgiving.

This prayer is also sometimes called "The Eucharistic Prayer," "The Great Prayer," "The Great Thanksgiving," and "The Prayer of Consecration." It is the central prayer of Christian worship, offered at the Table of the Lord's Supper. It begins with the traditional responses of the Sursum Corda.

Its structure is often broadly trinitarian, the first section praising God for mighty acts of creation and deliverance; the second remembering specifically the life, death, and resurrection of Jesus Christ; and the third invoking the power of the Holy Spirit. The middle section is bracketed by responses sung by the congregation: "Holy, Holy, Holy" (the Sanctus) and the Acclamation.

The prayer serves as a rehearsal of salvation history, not simply remembering God's mighty acts in the past, but also affirming that worshipers stand in the stream of God's history and can look for God's redemptive acts today. Past, present, and future all find expression in this prayer. Remembering what God has done, we are aware of what God is doing, and alert to what God will yet do, in Jesus Christ who was crucified, is risen, and will come again.

The Lord's Prayer traditionally follows the Great Prayer of Thanksgiving. (*See also* Acclamation; Lord's Prayer; Lord's Supper; Salvation History; Sanctus; Sursum Corda.)

Healing Service.

See Service for Wholeness.

Holy Saturday.

This day is observed in silence by many Christians since there is nothing said about it in scripture. It was, of course, the Sabbath for the followers of Jesus, a time for them to abstain from all work and to reflect on God's grace and mighty deliverance.

Christian observance of Holy Saturday often takes this same course, a quiet reflection on the paradox of Good Friday and the wondrous grace of God's act of redemption in Jesus Christ.

Holy Saturday ends with the Easter Vigil, which looks forward to the joyous celebration of Easter Day. (*See also* Easter Vigil; Good Friday.)

Holy Spirit.

Holy Spirit is a name. Often we refer to "*the* Holy Spirit," but using the definite article can make the Holy Spirit sound like a thing rather than a person. Sometimes it is better not to use the definite article, to help us get used to thinking in more personal terms. For Holy Spirit is very personal, the most intimate way God comes to us individually and corporately.

Holy Spirit is the giver of life itself and the one who gives us new life in Jesus Christ. Some say it is like being "born again" when Holy Spirit breathes in one's soul.

God gives gifts through Holy Spirit. We are inspired to be God's servants in a variety of ways through the "charisms" of God's Spirit.

The greatest gift we receive is that of unity. We belong to God, we are all redeemed by Jesus Christ, and in a real sense we are bound to one another. The glue that holds us together is Holy Spirit. The awareness that we are together in Christ's love is Holy Spirit. The sense that each of us is part of something much larger than any or all of us could imagine is also Holy Spirit.

Holy Spirit is like breath in each of us. Most of the time we are not conscious of breathing, and most of the time we are not conscious of the work of God's Holy Spirit, breathing the new life of Christ in us. Holy Spirit is always there, helping us to be more than we could ever be by ourselves.

As often as not, we are unaware of Holy Spirit's presence in worship. Holy Spirit blows through our worship sometimes like a raging storm but mostly as a gentle breeze. Holy Spirit inspires (literally "breathes into") us with something of

God. We are moved, in the sense of being prodded, into new attitudes and new behavior. We are also moved in the sense of being touched deeply both in emotion and understanding.

God's Holy Spirit inspires or moves us at moments we might expect—in an anthem sung by the choir that lifts our hearts, in a sermon that has just the right words to touch us deeply, in the baptism of a new life claimed by God, or in the sharing of bread, the Body of Christ, with a stranger in the pew. There are also moments when Holy Spirit surprises us—as we leaf through the Bible and discover a word or phrase speaking to our heart, as a friend smiles at us from across the aisle, or as a child laughs. When we come to church on the Lord's Day, we expect God to be with us—Father, Son, and Holy Spirit. We should especially expect to be touched by Holy Spirit. If we come with anticipation and expectation, then we will be alert worshipers, ready to rejoice and respond when God's breath is breathed into us once again. (*See also* Charism/Charismata/Charismatic; Epiclesis; Father, Son, and Holy Spirit; Language of Worship.)

Holy Week.

The idea of observing the week before Easter as a special time for worship dates from the middle of the third century although it did not develop fully for another hundred years. Palm Sunday, Good Friday, and then Maundy Thursday made their appearance as the events of Christ's last days were linked with certain days of the week.

The events of Holy Week find a chronology as early as the Gospel of Mark, where the scheme is as follows:

Palm Sunday: Entry into Jerusalem (Mark 11:1–11)

Holy Monday: Cursing the fig tree and cleansing the Temple (11:12–19)

Holy Tuesday: Jesus' teaching at the Temple (11:20–13:37)

Holy Wednesday: Jesus anointed in Bethany and Judas's Betrayal (14:1–11)

Maundy Thursday: The Last Supper, arrest, and trial (14:12–72)

Good Friday: Trial, crucifixion, and burial (15:1–47)

Holy Saturday: Jesus in the tomb (no text)

Easter Sunday: Resurrection (16:1–8)

In current practice, Holy Week is observed mainly by worship on Palm Sunday, Maundy Thursday, Good Friday, and Easter Vigil. Appropriate observance of Holy Week reminds the worshiper of the sorrow and mystery of the crucifixion that comes between the Palm Sunday celebration and the Easter rejoicing.

The days of Holy Week set the tone for the prayers of the people on the days of every week, just as Easter sets the tone for Sunday worship. Wednesday, the day of betrayal, calls for Christians to ask themselves, "Is it I, Lord?" Thursday is the day of learning, listening to the commandments of Jesus Christ as the disciples did on Maundy Thursday. Friday is the day of crucifixion, and so Christian piety turns to reflect on the mystery of the cross. Friday is, in some traditions, considered a fast day for this reason. Saturday, the Sabbath, is a day for quiet renewal. (*See also* Easter; Easter Vigil; Good Friday; Lent; Maundy Thursday; Palm Sunday; Pascha; Passion Sunday.)

Homily.

Roman Catholics generally use this term for sermon, while Protestants opt for the word "sermon." The two words mean the same thing, namely the proclamation of the Word. Sometimes the term is inaccurately used to mean something less than a sermon, either in duration or quality. A homily is not a minisermon nor a devotional sharing. It is a sermon. (*See also* Preaching/Proclaiming the Word.)

Hymn.

A hymn is a song of praise to God but also may include elements of proclamation and prayer. Hymns of the church fall into general historical groupings.

Biblical. The Psalms are representative of the hymnody of the Hebrew Scriptures. They are, for the most part, prayers, meant to be sung. They were compiled into a "hymnbook" for the Second Temple. There are other Hebrew canticles as well such as the Song of Moses and the Song of Miriam in Exodus 15.

In the New Testament we find considerable evidence for the singing of hymns and songs of faith in worship (see Eph. 5:19, Col. 3:16, and 1 Cor. 14:15). The songs of Mary, Zechariah, and Simeon—the Magnificat (Luke 1:46–55), Benedictus (Luke 1:68–79), and Nunc Dimittis (Luke 2:29–32)—are examples of such hymnody that has found traditional places in the structure of daily prayer. Other New Testament hymns that were apparently sung in early Christian worship are found in Philippians 2:5–11 and Colossians 1:15–20.

Early Church and Middle Ages. During the first three centuries persecution sometimes drove the Christian church underground to worship in secret. This setting inhibited singing. However, with the Edict of Milan in 313, Christianity was officially recognized by the state. Ambrose (c. 339–97), the bishop of Milan, composed several hymns still used today (for example, "Savior of the Nations, Come" and "O Splendor of God's Glory Bright"). Pope Gregory I (540–604) became the patron of a type of chanting known as "plainsong," characterized by a simple and plain melody line with no strict meter to fit the text (thus "Gregorian chant"). Throughout the Middle Ages chanting was done by those in religious orders and by the clergy. It became increasingly complicated to sing, so the people were less and less involved.

Reformation. The period of the Reformation was characterized by two trends sponsored by major figures of Protestantism. Martin Luther (1483–1546) gave singing back to the people, matching vigorous texts with chorale tunes having strong melody lines. "A Mighty Fortress Is Our God" is a prime example.

John Calvin (1509–64) also encouraged the development

of hymnody by the setting of metrical psalms and hymns to singable tunes written by his friend Louis Bourgeois (c.1510–61). The tune "Old Hundredth" is attributed to Bourgeois, and provides a setting for Psalm 100. Calvin advocated a return to the simplicity of the early church. Thus the hymns, though of human authorship, were biblically based to nurture the people's piety. Psalmody was the preferred singing for a Reformed congregation at worship.

Post-Reformation. In the late sixteenth century and into the seventeenth, metrical hymns were increasingly popular. People took more interest in singing in worship, and gradually a body of popular hymns developed in a number of collections. By the eighteenth century people were ready for an explosion of hymnody by Isaac Watts (1674–1748), John Wesley (1703–1791), and Charles Wesley (1707–1788). Watts was convinced that hymns need not conform strictly to paraphrases of biblical texts but should break free and praise God in expressions of the common thoughts and feelings of the people. His hymns were related to the emphasis of the sermon. Standard metrical forms were employed in short, long, and common meter. "Joy to the World!" is one of the most familiar of Watts's hymns. Charles Wesley was the writer of hymns and his brother John the promoter, making sure that Charles's hymns received wide distribution and publication. A well-known example of Charles Wesley's hymns is "Christ the Lord Is Risen Today!"

Nineteenth Century. Following the Wesleys and Watts came a period characterized by romanticism. This was displayed in two ways. First, hymn tunes of this period were dependent on harmony to make them work, and the melodies were chromatic. The texts were of literary quality, often written by famous poets, and often very subjective and personal in content. "Dear Lord and Father of Mankind" is a perfect example.

The other emphasis in this period was on translations of ancient hymns, going along with a romantic interest in archaeology and the ancient past. John Mason Neale and Katherine Winkworth were two hymn writers of this period who sought to reclaim the piety of earlier days with their translations. See "All Glory, Laud, and Honor," translated by Neale; and "Now Thank We All Our God," translated by Winkworth.

Twentieth Century. Hymns of the twentieth century are characterized by their complexity, both structurally and musically. An outstanding example of this kind of hymn is "For All the Saints."

Contemporary. Contemporary hymns may borrow from or follow in the style of secular music. The Doxology and Gloria by Richard Avery and Donald Marsh are examples. Old folk tunes are often recycled; for example, "I Danced in the Morning," by Sydney Carter, recasts a Shaker melody.

Hymns are often selected for worship by the pastor in consultation with church musicians. Criteria often applied in choosing hymns include the following:

1. The hymn should focus on the praise of God rather than on human feelings or experiences.
2. The hymn should be faithful to scripture, and a hymn based on a biblical text should not distort its meaning or add ideas to it.
3. The hymn should be reverent in language, not banal or trivial.
4. The text of the hymn should be good poetry.
5. The hymn should be structurally sound, coherent, with organic and conceptual unity.
6. The hymn should appeal to the common experience of the congregation.
7. The tune should be singable.
8. The tune should be consistent with the mood of the text.
9. The tune should fit the text and enhance its meaning.

Much can be learned about a hymn from a brief look at the hymnal page itself. In the Presbyterian hymnal, for example, the author or source of the text is given on the upper left side of the page and the composer or source of the tune on the right. The title of the tune is given under the title of the hymn text, usually its first line. The meter of the text is also indicated either by numbers or by abbreviations that indicate the number of syllables in each line of text. "C.M." means "common meter," so named because it is the most commonly used meter, having eight syllables in the first line, six in the second, eight in the third, and six in the fourth (8.6.8.6.). "S.M." means "short meter," namely 6.6.8.6., and "L.M." means "long meter," namely 8.8.8.8. "D." means doubled, so "C.M.D." would indicate a hymn of eight lines having syllables as follows: 8.6.8.6.8.6.8.6. Some hymns follow a unique pattern and are noted as "Irregular," such as "O Come, All Ye Faithful" ("Adeste Fideles"). Hymns can be sung to other tunes with that same meter. Changing the tune may result in a different impact of the text. Note, for example, that "O Little Town of Bethlehem" can be set to "Forest Green" or "St. Louis." (*See also* Canticle; Choir; Congregation; Psalms; Song; Spirituals.)

Imposition of Ashes.

See Ash Wednesday.

Incense.

Incense is resin from certain trees that gives off an aromatic smoke when burned. "Frankincense," which was offered as a gift to the Christ-child, is simply incense from a particular type of East African and Arabian tree (genus *Boswellia*).

Incense was used in biblical times. Psalm 141:2 suggests that prayers rise up to God as the fragrance of incense. The Revelation of John gives a picture of worship with the smoke of incense mingling with the prayers of the people (Rev. 8:3–4).

During the first three centuries, the Christian church did not use incense, probably as a reaction to its use in pagan culture and its association with emperor worship. In the fourth century, incense began to be used broadly, particularly during the Lord's Supper. Calvin and other Reformers abandoned incense along with the rest of the Mass, returning to primitive practices that did not include incense.

The use of incense in Protestant churches is rare although in recent years the practice has been given new consideration. It is simply a symbol for prayer, appealing to the sense of smell to suggest that our prayers should rise to please God. Roman Catholic, Orthodox, and Episcopal churches do use incense, particularly on such special occasions as Christmas, Easter, and ordinations.

All the senses are involved in worship. Obviously, we see and hear. We touch hymnals, the texture of wood in pews, and the people around us in greeting. With the Lord's Supper we smell and taste the bread and wine. We also smell the fragrance of flowers as well as odors of the building, cleaning materials, and people's perfumes. The sense of smell is very powerful in recalling experiences. The use of incense provides a specific fragrance to be associated with prayer and can be a rich symbol, reminding us of prayers ascending to God. (*See also* Gospel; Prayer.)

Inclusive Language.

See Language of Worship.

Icons.

See Art.

Institution, Words of.

The words of institution of the Lord's Supper are found in Paul's First Letter to the Corinthians 11:23–26. This text, or a liturgical modification, is almost universally used to introduce the Lord's Supper and is considered essential to the sacrament. In Reformed worship, the text is cited in the liturgy as Jesus' command to his disciples, and therefore to us, about the breaking and eating of the bread and the sharing of the cup. It is recited at one of the following places: a) at the begin-

ning of the Lord's Supper, b) in the Great Prayer of Thanksgiving, or c) at the breaking of the bread and sharing the cup
by the minister.

One of the criteria for a "sacrament" is that it is explicitly
commanded by Christ. The words of institution constitute
that command, standing as a warrant for the celebration of
the Lord's Supper. (*See also* Lord's Supper; Great Prayer of
Thanksgiving; Sacrament.)

Intercession.

Intercession is simply prayer for others, as distinguished
from petition, which is prayer for ourselves, yet they have
much in common. Recognizing that we have needs, we can
surmise that others do too. In fact, in the community of faith
we become well aware of the needs of others, those we know
in our church or community and people around the world.

When we pray for others, we claim God's promises of love
and power for them. One might ask, does not God already
know the needs of others, just as our own needs are known
before we begin to pray? The answer, of course, is yes. God
does know human needs. Our prayers of intercession are not
so much to remind God of human needs but to remember
them ourselves as we connect with God's power.

When we pray for others, we make a commitment before
God to be God's agents in the answering of those prayers.
When we pray, for example, for the victims of natural disas-
ters, we are making a commitment to reach out to them with
our physical and material help. Prayer for others is never an
abstraction but takes shape in our own persons and actions.

Intercessory prayers in Christian worship are sometimes
called "the prayers of the people" or the "pastoral prayer."
The point is that the prayers reflect the needs and concerns of
the people of the church, even if they are verbalized by the
pastor. Sometimes people from the congregation may suggest
needs as the subjects of prayer or even articulate brief prayers.
When this is done, care should be given that all can hear.

A useful form of intercessory prayer is the "bidding

prayer," with the leader bidding the congregation to pray for a series of needs, each to be followed by a period of silence and a summary prayer to which the congregation responds with a set phrase. "The Solemn Intercession" is a series of bidding prayers. This was originally the form of the prayers of the people in the Roman Catholic Church, but it is now used only on Good Friday. Some litanies may also be useful as intercessory prayers.

The content for intercessions will vary from time to time as circumstances require. Yet there are several topics that are commonly included, usually beginning with the broadest scope and narrowing the focus to the more particular and immediate.

The world: The peoples and nations of the world struggle, often violently, and deserve our prayerful concern. World leaders need our prayers for strength and wisdom to find peaceful solutions to problems.

The church: Prayers for the world church of Jesus Christ should be offered each week as a reminder that each congregation is part of a larger whole. It is helpful to particularize these prayers to include neighboring congregations of other denominations on a rotating basis.

Our country: The President, Congress, and courts of our land should be regularly remembered in prayer, with others who are in state and local governments, so they may guide us according to God's will and we may be responsible citizens.

The poor: Those who are impoverished, the homeless, and hungry always need our concern, and praying for them encourages us to meet their needs, starting in our own community.

The sick: Those who are ill in hospital or home should be remembered, members of the church community by name, and others generally or in a time of silence when worshipers supply the names of those they know. Prayers are also appropriate for those who give immediate care for the sick—physicians, nurses, aides, technicians, and family members.

The bereaved: Those who grieve over the loss of a loved one need the support of friends in faith. Intercessions remind us all of those needs so we may give our presence to help meet their emptiness.

One another: The congregation will pray for one another, remembering the unspoken needs and concerns brought to worship by the people. This becomes the foundation for a supportive community of people caring for one another in concrete ways.

(*See also* Bidding Prayer; Mission; Pastoral Care; Prayer.)

Introit.

See Call to Worship.

Invocation.

The use of the term *invocation* in Christian worship can be confusing. Technically the term refers to the invoking (*epiclesis*) of the Holy Spirit in the prayers of the sacraments, claiming God's promised power. Popularly, it is used to describe the opening prayer of a meeting or a worship service.

The problem comes when an invocation is given at the beginning of Lord's Day worship, for this implies that God's presence is being invoked. Are we inviting God to our worship service? Surely this is the wrong way around, for are we not called to worship by God? It is not "our" worship service, for God summons the people of God to worship and service. We are present at God's invitation issued through the grace of our Lord Jesus Christ. The first prayer of the service might better be labeled "Prayer of Adoration" or simply "Opening Prayer." The "Prayer for the Day," one that is related to seasonal or lectionary themes, might be used as the congregation gathers.

Invocations may be appropriate at civil or secular meetings where people gather on their own initiative rather than God's. While God is omnipresent, at a secular meeting the divine presence may be invoked by way of acknowledgment. There is, however, a potential problem here as well, for the invocation of God's presence at a public meeting may seem to be sanctifying whatever happens there. It is better in these situations to avoid the term "invocation" and settle for an "opening prayer." Similarly, instead of a "benediction" one might just offer a "closing prayer." (*See also* Benediction; Epiclesis; Great Prayer of Thanksgiving; Prayer for the Day.)

Jesus Christ.

Jesus Christ is the Word of God. When God spoke, it was not in abstractions. God said "Let there be . . . ," and creation happened in a material and physical way. God spoke love, and Jesus Christ happened, the new creation in flesh and blood (John 1:1–14).

Jesus Christ is risen, and our worship stands firmly on that fact. We worship on the day of resurrection, and we expect to meet the risen Lord. The Christian quorum is two or three, for when we gather in the name of Jesus Christ, he is there in our midst (Matt. 18:20). Jesus Christ is present in the world in his body, which is the church. Those who respond to God's call to worship become the body of Christ, his hands to bring healing, his feet to follow pathways of peace, his voice to speak truth and justice.

Jesus Christ is the one in whose name we approach God. He becomes our mediator, our advocate before the throne of the Almighty. Prayers often end with a formulaic statement such as, "in the name of Jesus Christ we pray."

The Bible from which we read attests to the Word God spoke in Jesus Christ. The sermon, as well, points to Christ, to introduce the listener to the living Lord. Baptism and the Lord's Supper show Christ present. While baptism reminds us that we are identified with Christ, it is in the regular breaking of bread in the Lord's Supper that our eyes are opened and we recognize Christ.

All of these liturgical acts go together to form a celebration of the Christ event: the birth, life, death, resurrection, and ascension of Jesus Christ. It is not a fond memory but a real presence that is celebrated. (*See also* Baptism; Bible/Scripture/Word of God; Lord's Supper; Lord's Day/Sunday/Sabbath; Preaching/Proclaiming the Word; Resurrection.)

Kerygma.

This Greek word means "proclamation by a herald." It signifies the essential Christian message, the core of the Good News, the primitive and pure message as preached by the apostles.

Paul summarized it in his First Letter to the Corinthians (15:3–5). This was the basic message that he had received and was passing on, the message of God's redemptive act in the death and resurrection of Jesus Christ.

The kerygma stands as a kind of beacon light to help us keep our bearings and not run aground on the rocks of theological complexity. The gospel is profound, but it is also simple. In order to be a Christian, one need not digest enormous quantities of doctrine. Only a simple statement of faith suffices: Jesus Christ died for the redemption of humankind and was raised from the dead so we all might live. Sometimes it is phrased in terms of "accepting Jesus Christ as one's Lord and Savior," but it means the same thing. We affirm Jesus Christ as Savior of the whole world, and we accept him personally as our Lord. Kerygma has both cosmic and personal significance.

It is the kerygma that provides an essential guide for preaching in the church. Paul emphasized it in this regard, saying that his only purpose was to preach Christ, and him crucified (1 Cor. 1:23–25 and 2:2). (*See also* Preaching/Proclaiming the Word; Resurrection.)

Koinonia.

This Greek word is usually translated "fellowship" and refers specifically to the fellowship of the Christian community.

There are many gatherings of people in this world, but there is none like the gathering of Christians into the fellowship of the church. In most groups people come together around common interests or concerns or for some mutual benefit. In the church people are gathered quite apart from common interests. In fact, it is the strength of the church that it includes a great diversity of perspective and ability. In most groups people gather voluntarily, and while we often think this is true of the church, in a deeper sense it is only by the compelling grace of God that we are brought into the community of faith. Most groups have self-interest in mind while the church is ready to give its life for others.

Gathered in koinonia, the church is strengthened in Jesus Christ and bound ever more closely together by the power of the Holy Spirit. This is a nurturing and healing experience, a time for renewal. The educational process of the church is part of its koinonia, as is pastoral care and the mutual caring of the members.

Koinonia finds its clearest expression in the meal shared in Jesus Christ at the Lord's Supper. Here as nowhere else, the church is nourished and fed by its risen Lord. Agape meals are also expressions of koinonia, as we break bread together and share one another's food.

Koinonia is only one end of a polarity, the other end of which is diakonia. We are gathered in the fellowship of the church to be strengthened to go out to be Christ's church in service. Diakonia and koinonia represent the gathering and scattering of the church, the coming and going that is the pulse of the church's life. (*See also* Agape Meal; Congregation; Diakonia; Mission.)

Kyrie.

Kyrie eleison is Greek for "Lord, have mercy," a petition sung in most historical liturgies, often in Greek. Originally it was a response used in a litany of intercessions and took on a three-part format ("Lord, have mercy upon us; Christ, have mercy upon us; Lord, have mercy upon us"), later magnified to a triple three-part format with each line sung three times. The simpler arrangement is most often used today. It has been suggested that the three-part format indicates that it is a trinitarian prayer, addressed to God the Father as Lord, Christ, and the Holy Spirit as Lord. This is probably not true, for historically the whole prayer has been used as addressed to Christ the Lord.

While its logical use is at the time of the prayer of confession, the "Kyrie" also serves well as a response to intercessory prayers. We seek the mercy of Christ even as we pray for the needs of others, for as we know Christ to be merciful in our lives, we claim Christ's mercy for others. Also, the prayer is a reminder to identify with the needs of others so that their sorrows and difficulties become ours and call forth our prayers and our actions. (*See also* Intercession, Prayers of; Confession of Sin.)

Laity/Lay Reader/Lay Leader.

The term *laity* comes from a Greek word meaning "people" and is used to refer to the people of God. A word often used for worship is *liturgy*, which carries within it this Greek root for people. Liturgy is defined as the work of the people.

Christian worship is an activity of the people and is to be understood in corporate rather than individual terms. Even when a solitary Christian worships, it is a corporate activity and includes the whole people of God. The individual always stands in the context of the church, for each is baptized into the body and numbered among the people of God.

The Reformation concept of "the priesthood of all believers" has bearing on our understanding of the people of God. The Reformers knew that worship belonged to the people, to all the people, and was not something performed by a few while the many watched. The priestly function of access to God was seen as open to all people; the priestly function of intercession to God on behalf of others was recognized as the mutual responsibility of all people. The implications of this for worship are several.

First, the clergy's role is changed from surrogate worshiper to leader of the people's worship. While the minister is ordained to specific functions of preaching and administering the sacraments, it is not an exclusive role but one performed on behalf of the whole church. The purpose of ordination is to guarantee that those essential functions will be performed, not to make them the exclusive prerogatives of a few. The role of the minister of Word and sacrament, then, is to serve the people's worship.

Second, the role of the congregation shifts from passive to active. No longer are the people expected to be spectators of worship; now they are to be participants.

Third, since the people are to be active participants in worship and clergy are to be leaders, the leadership is rightfully shared among clergy and nonclergy. Only preaching and administration of the sacraments are the designated responsibilities of the clergy. Leading in prayers, reading scripture, providing music, and other leadership tasks may be done by people from the congregation. In this way, the participation of the whole people is made visible in the leadership of their representatives.

A common practice in Protestant and Roman Catholic churches is to have lay readers of scripture in Lord's Day worship. This is a dramatic symbol of the Reformation's emphasis on providing the Bible in the language of the people. Hearing the scripture read by one of the congregation reminds us that the Word of God revealed in the Bible speaks to and through each of God's people. It is also a reminder that the Bible is to be read regularly by all the people.

Some training is necessary for those who will lead in worship. While the clergy are trained to speak in public and to read scripture with meaning, this is often difficult for others who are willing and even eager to give their leadership to worship. Therefore, it is only fair that they receive some instruction and practice in advance. Furthermore, preparation of lay readers is essential for the sake of effectiveness in reading scripture and communicating its message in worship. Not only speaking techniques but also an appropriate sense of awe and reverence in approaching the task should be emphasized.

Lay leadership in worship should be broadly shared, so

that many people in the congregation may have the experience. It challenges them to grow in faith and to share in a special way with their co-worshipers. The more people have such leadership experiences in a congregation, the more all the people will have a sense of commonality in their worship.

The active involvement of all the people in worship has meant that through the centuries various cultural forms have been appropriated for Christian worship. Music from the culture is often enlisted for liturgical purposes, as folk tunes and even popular melodies are adopted as vehicles for religious texts. This is one of the ways liturgy grows and has vitality. Traditions are begun as well as continued, and even ancient liturgical acts are renovated so that they are useful in modern settings.

Lay leadership in worship is also indicative of the lay ministries that are conducted by the people outside the walls of the church. When people from the congregation share in leading worship, they become a visible symbol of the fullness of Christian ministry that requires all the people's participation. (*See also* Bible/Scripture/Word of God; Hymn; Liturgy; Minister; Ordination.)

Language of Worship.

One definition of worship comes from the word *liturgy*, literally "the work of the people." Worship is what all the people of God do as they come together to praise and serve God in response to God's call.

The language of worship, then, must be contemporary language since the words of the liturgy are in the people's mouths. Beginning in the late 1960s, worshiping congregations largely abandoned the archaic phrasing and vocabulary of seventeenth-century English. The language of liturgy had reflected the King James Version of the Bible. With the advent of new and popular translations, liturgical expression needed to change. The "thee" and "thou" of the old way, along with many standard phrases and expressions, had become stilted and empty. Twentieth-century people need an up-to-date English for their worship.

The 1960s and 1970s were a time for experimentation in worship, especially in language. Often the language of worship was trendy or faddish. The pendulum had swung the other way, from stilted and formal-sounding language to a folksy and often pedestrian style. Worship suffered, many thought, from a lack of dignity. For them, at least the language of the King James Bible sounded dignified.

More recently, serious efforts have been given to the production of sound liturgical texts in English. Several denominations (including the Presbyterians, Methodists, Episcopalians, Lutherans, and Roman Catholics) have published resources and service books that offer fine liturgies for the Lord's Day worship as well as for baptisms, weddings, funerals, daily prayer, and pastoral care situations. These resources have attempted to find language that fits comfortably in the mouths of contemporary people and yet has dignity and quality.

As liturgical English of the past was shaped by the King James Version of the Bible, so modern liturgical language finds its cues in modern biblical translations. The secret is that liturgical language is biblical language. Do you want to know how to pray? Pray for yourself the Psalms and other prayers of the Bible, and you will learn. The language we use for worship shows how well we have studied the scripture, insofar as it reflects biblical imagery and phrases. Solid modern translations, such as *The New Revised Standard Version*, *The New English Bible*, and *The New Jerusalem Bible*, are all helpful in this regard.

Our approach to God is shaped by the rich imagery in scripture. God is not only "Father," for example, but also appears in maternal images (such as Exod. 19:4 where God is pictured as a mother eagle supporting her fledglings in flight). Jesus also applied a maternal image to himself (Matt. 23:37). God defies our description, so all our images are but metaphors that reach in God's direction.

The language of liturgy relating to people is also rich and avoids stereotypes. "Inclusiveness" is a word we hear often, meaning that our language should never exclude anyone from the worship of God. Generic masculine terms tend to exclude women and are to be avoided so as not to give offence. Good liturgy does not call attention to itself but points foremost to God. In our prayers, creeds, hymns, and anthems, we praise God as fully as we can with all God's people, using the best language we have at our disposal. (*See also* Bible/Scripture/Word of God; Father, Son, and Holy Spirit.)

Laying on of Hands.

Touch is a very important aspect of relationships and is significant in our relationship with God. The laying on of hands is a gesture of significance in worship for it becomes a tangible symbol of God's touch for us.

Ordination. In ordination, hands of church authorities are placed on the head of one being ordained, signifying the transmittal of authority and the sharing of responsibility. As such, the action serves to set apart some people for particular roles in the church.

The laying on of hands, however, also includes a blessing, probably the most traditional meaning for this gesture. For if there is authority and responsibility, there are also gifts from God that will enable the person to fulfill his or her role.

Laying on of hands in ordination also communicates the continuity of the church, as clergy are ordained in the "apostolic succession" to proclaim the apostolic faith, elders are ordained by their predecessors in governing, and deacons are ordained to continue their vital ministry of serving.

At ordinations, the hands of many are laid on a few, and the weight can be heavy, which itself is a symbol of the weighty responsibility ordination involves.

Baptism. In baptism, the gesture of laying on of hands is a blessing on the baptized person, claiming him or her for

God's very own. Baptism may be thought of as the basic ordination of all Christians, and laying on of hands in the sacrament communicates the transmission of authority and
responsibility to the new disciple.

In baptism, laying on of hands is also associated with
anointing. The two together clearly indicate the person is
claimed and empowered to be a disciple of the Anointed One
of God.

Confirmation. In confirmation, laying on of hands helps recall baptism and carries the additional emphasis of acknowledging that the person enters upon a mature and responsible
participation in the faith community. It is the affirmation of
the basic ordination of baptism, and includes emphasis on the
disciple's commitment to follow Christ in ministry.

Pastoral Care. The laying on of hands also has a healing significance. The blessing of God communicated by this gesture
is one that brings peace for the brokenness of the soul. It is a
sign of the forgiveness of sin and especially of the restored
relationship between God and the person.

Touch is important in pastoral care, and the laying on of
hands has theological content. It is not simply the touch of
the pastor's hand on the person, but through the pastor's
touch the support of the entire fellowship and the renewing
grace of Jesus Christ are offered. It is the touch of Christ,
communicated by the representative of the physical body of
Christ, the church. (*See also* Anointing; Baptism; Confirmation; Gesture and Posture; Ordination; Pastoral Care.)

Lectern.

The lectern is a stand to hold a book—the Bible or a prayer
book—for public reading. It is to be distinguished from the pulpit, the desk from which the sermon is given, although in many
Reformed churches one stand is used for both functions.

When the lectern, not the pulpit, holds the Bible, the message is that preaching is not the same as reading scripture. If
the pulpit is larger and higher, it may suggest that preaching

is considered more important. When the pulpit is also the lectern holding the Bible, the message is that preaching is to be based on scripture. In this instance, a separate lectern may be used for the leading of the prayers and the rest of the service. (*See also* Bible/Scripture/Word of God; Pulpit.)

Lectionary.

A lectionary is a schedule of scripture readings set out for use in worship for a year or more. The term may also be used to refer to a book containing those readings for use in worship services.

Many clergy welcome the lectionary as a discipline that encourages them to wrestle with the human issues posed in scripture. Also a systematic approach to scripture reading enables lay people to be aware of the schedule, read the lessons in advance, and come to participate in the sermon as prepared listeners. Another advantage of a lectionary is that in the course of a three-year cycle it presents the major themes of the Bible.

Other clergy do not want to be bound to a lectionary that arbitrarily dictates what Scripture should be used. They feel that the preacher should be free to respond to current issues in the life of the congregation and open to the movement of the Spirit. A set schedule of Scripture readings from which to preach inhibits homiletical flexibility.

There are basically two kinds of lectionaries: continual readings of Scripture passages in sequence (*lectio continua*), and selected readings according to the Christian year or Sunday thematic emphasis (*lectio selecta*).

The Reformers opted for continual, sequential readings. This kind of lectionary had the advantage of enabling a series of sermons on one book of the Bible, for example, in which a biblical theme could be explored in some depth with greater exposition. The responsibility of the minister as "teaching elder" was emphasized. Also, the Reformers tended to distrust celebration of the Christian year, so a lectionary influenced by the calendar was suspect as well.

In modern times the selective lectionary has gained in popularity, especially the Common Lectionary adopted by many major denominations. Advocates of this lectionary point to its ecumenical strength: the worship of Christians gains a common focus each week in the scripture, bringing the churches together on the solid foundation of the Bible. Furthermore, they find the celebration of the Christian year to be beneficial, and the set lessons support this. Also they assert the benefit of discipline for the preacher and the ability of churchgoers to prepare to participate in the sermon by advance study of the text.

Often a preacher who uses a lectionary approach will decide to abandon it for a week or more because of peculiar circumstances in the congregation's life or needs of the people, or to preach a series of sermons on a theme or book of the Bible. Even the Common Lectionary has sequential readings (although they are not always continuous), thus providing a combination of the two approaches that allows for a sermon series working through a given book.

The use of a lectionary as the basis for preaching tends to promote expository preaching that explains the biblical text and relates it to contemporary living. Those who preach topical sermons that explore a topic or subject rather than a text will make less use of a lectionary because texts will need to be selected as they apply to the topic at hand.

Lectionaries are also devised for daily use, usually on a two-year cycle (see the *Lutheran Book of Worship*, the Episcopal *Book of Common Prayer*, and the Presbyterian and Reformed *Daily Prayer*). These often include longer readings than those selected for Sunday morning on the premise that they are not foundations for sermons but are to be used as the focus of personal meditation. A three-year cycle Sunday lectionary is also easily adaptable for daily use.

It has been traditional in Christian worship to have three texts read each Sunday: Old Testament (Hebrew Scripture), New Testament epistle, and Gospel. The three may or may not be interrelated. On Sundays with seasonal or special emphasis they tend to be related but not on other Sundays. It is important to have all three readings so as to proclaim the fullness of the biblical message and provide an adequate context for the sermon's text.

A psalm often follows the Old Testament (Hebrew Scripture) reading, not as another reading, but as a congregational response of sung prayer to the Old Testament. The Common Lectionary includes a schedule for using the Psalms in Lord's Day worship. (*See also* Bible/Scripture/Word of God; Daily Prayer; Ecumenism; Lesson; Preaching/Proclaiming the Word; Psalms.)

Lent.

A period of forty days (not counting Sundays) before Easter, Lent was originally a period of preparation for those to be baptized at Easter. It later became a time of penitence for all Christians. Thus, it emulated the forty days Jesus spent in the wilderness preparing for his ministry, resisting temptations. Christians often fast or give up various things during Lent to remind themselves of Christ's sacrifice and to overcome destructive habits. Christians may also take on disciplines as they learn new habits that are constructive and useful for disciples of Jesus Christ. Lent begins with Ash Wednesday and includes the days of Holy Week. The color for Lent is purple. (*See also* Ash Wednesday; Holy Week; Lord's Day/Sunday/Sabbath.)

Lesson (Scripture).

A scripture reading is often referred to as a "lesson," suggesting there is instruction involved. While preaching is not the same as teaching, there is certainly an educational aspect to the proclamation of the gospel. From the beginning, followers of Christ have been called "disciples," which literally means "learners." Jesus was known as "Rabbi," or "teacher." When the scripture was read in the synagogue, the lessons of the passage were taught. Christians have maintained this connection of teaching with preaching and learning with discipleship.

The use of the black academic robe by Reformed preachers is an indication of the premium placed on this role of the clergy. The Geneva bands or tabs sometimes worn signify the tablets of the Law and are a sign of the responsibility of the clergy to be teachers of the Law of God. (*See also* Discipline; Pastor; Preaching/Proclaiming the Word; Vestments/Robes/Stoles.)

Litany.

A litany is a form of prayer that includes a refrain-type response by the congregation. It may be a series of petitions, leading the congregation's prayer about certain things, or it may be simply a prayer in which the congregation responds with a closing line to each petition.

Litanies are often used because they involve the congregation more directly in the prayers. When worshipers vocalize a response in a prayer, they tend to concentrate more on the prayer's content. What is more, they will supply their own specific content to the prayer's more general petitions.

Another advantage of the litany format is that it allows a number of items to be covered without the prayer becoming tedious in length. Even if it is a longer prayer than usual, its short sections enable people to maintain concentration. (*See also* Prayer.)

Liturgy.

Liturgy is based on Greek words meaning literally "the work of the people." The word itself is a reminder that worship is work and that the people's role is not meant to be passive.

Liturgy in its broadest sense is a synonym for worship, referring specifically to corporate worship of Christians. In a narrower sense, liturgy refers to the words of worship, the prayers, responses, and songs of the people.

Sometimes worship is categorized as being "liturgical," "highly liturgical," or "nonliturgical," but these are false categories. All worship is liturgical in the sense of being the work of the people. How well a worship experience succeeds in fulfilling the definition of liturgy determines whether it is good or bad liturgy. All worship is liturgical, but all worship is not necessarily good liturgy.

The modern renewal of liturgy in Christian churches has taken place on several fronts. First, there has been a greater awareness of the value of visual aids to worship in symbols, colors, vestments, and gestures. This is in contrast to the austere Puritan streak in the Reformed tradition that bleached all color from places of worship and intellectualized the experience. Second, there has been an increase in the sense of drama in proclamation of the gospel. Preaching has received a new vitality, and music has rediscovered its role in announcing the Good News. Third, classic prayers from the full range of Christian heritage have been revived while new prayers of high quality and biblical tone have been composed, enabling worshipers to find words better to express their intimate praise to God. This has helped free and spontaneous prayer to be less wordy and trite as well. Finally, the use of lectionaries, especially the Common Lectionary, and the following of the Christian year have given an understandable structure to the worship of the people over a period of time. This has contributed much to the church's awareness of worship as a journey with Christ through life.

The movement toward liturgical renewal is an ecumenical effort directed at the renewal of the whole church of Jesus Christ. It therefore deals with substantive theological issues, such as the nature of the church, how the community of the faithful lives in its gathered life, the content of the church's proclamation, the significance of the sacraments, and the church's understanding and celebration of time. The purpose of renewing liturgy, then, is not simply for the sake of good worship, but for the sake of the whole life of the church. All efforts at renewal need to be evaluated in this light.

One result of renewal, already evident, is that liturgy is becoming more biblically rooted. This is not only to say that liturgy is using more biblical language or imagery, which may be true, but more important, it suggests that all denominations are responding to the people's need to have an adequate liturgical means to respond to God's call for a servant people, in the company of the risen Christ, empowered by the Holy Spirit. (*See also* Christian Year; Colors; Gesture and Posture; Lectionary; Symbols; Vestments/Robes/Stoles; Worship.)

Lord's Day/Sunday/Sabbath.

The Lord's Day is Sunday, sometimes referred to as "the Christian Sabbath." Its significance, however, is more complex than that. The first Christians were Jews, as was Jesus, who kept the Jewish Sabbath on the seventh day of the week. The Sabbath was kept as a day of rest, remembering God's gift of the whole creation and life itself, how God rested on the seventh day and blessed the Sabbath, and God's command (see Exod. 20:8–11). The Sabbath was also kept in honor of the redemptive act of God's deliverance of Israel from bondage (see Deut. 5:12–15).

Because the followers of Jesus kept the Jewish Sabbath, the burial of Jesus had to be hurried before the Sabbath began, and preparations of the body could not be completed until after the Sabbath was over. After the followers of Jesus encountered Christ risen from the grave, the first day of the week took on new meaning. The first day of the week, the day of resurrection, became known as the Lord's Day. Later the name "Sunday" was used, "the day of the sun" being appropriate for the day of resurrection. From the beginning, Sunday, the Lord's Day, was observed as a resurrection day and carried heavy festal and celebrative overtones. Sunday is the basis for the cycle of Christian worship.

Jewish Christians in all likelihood continued to observe both: the Sabbath as a day of rest from work, and the Lord's Day as a time to celebrate Christ's resurrection. When non-Jewish people became Christians, their observance of the Jewish Sabbath as such diminished. In time it was abandoned altogether by Christians. Calvin and other Reformers understood the Sabbath of the Jews to be replaced by the Lord's

Day of the Christians. The Sabbath was the Jewish day, the Lord's Day was for Christians.

In sixteenth-century Puritanism, however, the Sabbath concept was applied to the Christian Lord's Day, giving rise to a sabbatarian notion in Christian worship. The Christian Sabbath became a time for refraining from all that would interfere with worship. Sabbatarian Christianity tends to deal mainly with prohibitions, what one cannot do on the Christian Sabbath. In modern times some Christians still make this emphasis. The negative perspective of the Christian Sabbath tends to invest relatively minor matters with major concern. It is appropriate to think of the Lord's Day as a "Sabbath" more in the sense of devoting time and energy to the praise of God in celebration of the resurrection of the Lord Jesus Christ. That should be the priority for the Lord's Day, and nothing should be allowed to interfere.

Easter began as an annual great festival celebrating God's redemptive acts in the death and resurrection of Jesus Christ. By the fourth century, Good Friday developed to emphasize the death, leaving Easter to stress the resurrection. As Lent developed, the resurrection theme of Easter still dominated the Sunday celebrations. In counting the forty days of Lent, therefore, Sundays are excluded, retaining this separation of themes with Lent concentrating on the passion of Christ and Lord's Day worship on the resurrection. Sundays are "in" Lent but not "of" Lent. Nevertheless, Sundays in Lent will necessarily carry some of the freight of the season because there are all too few weekday opportunities for dealing with its themes. Therefore the Lord's Day celebration will inevitably be affected by the Lenten context.

Funeral services may be appropriate on Sunday precisely because it is the Lord's Day and a funeral is supposed to be a witness to the resurrection. At any rate, whenever a death occurs in the Christian community, thanksgiving may be given for the person's life and intercessions offered for the person's family at Lord's Day worship. (*See also* Easter; Funeral; Lent; Resurrection.)

Lord's Prayer.

Jesus taught his followers about prayer and gave an example of what their prayers should be like in what we call "The Lord's Prayer." It appears in the Sermon on the Mount as recorded in Matthew 6:9–13, and again in a shorter form in Luke 11:2–4. Luke's version does not include the final doxology, which is also missing in many manuscripts of Matthew.

The prayer is of a standard rabbinical type that would have been given in instruction to disciples by a Jewish teacher. While the doxology at the end of Matthew's version suggests its early use in Christian worship, it was not commonly used until the end of the fourth century. From that time on it was used universally.

The Lord's Prayer is historically placed in the context of the Lord's Supper, the reference to "daily bread" being the obvious connection. Sometimes it is placed early in the service as a part of the preparation to hear the Word proclaimed in scripture and sermon. The petition for forgiveness makes it appropriate here, and the "daily bread" can be understood to apply both to the Word in scripture and sermon and to the Word revealed in the sacrament (Jesus said, "I am the bread of life" [John 6:35]). The Lord's Prayer has been useful from the early centuries as an essential element of daily prayer.

The Lord's Prayer is a model for prayer. It was probably not intended to be used as we use it today, spoken in unison. Nevertheless, its regular use in Christian worship makes it a part of people's memories, so they can employ it at any time as a springboard for their own prayers. It is one of those things we learn by heart through sheer usage, rather than by a conscious memorization process. Children often learn the prayer even before they know what all the words mean, and as they grow older the prayer has long since become a part of them as they begin to appreciate its content.

Presbyterians and some other Protestants use the Lord's Prayer found in the King James Version of the Bible with its reference to "debts" and "debtors." Other Christians use a different version with "trespasses" and "those who trespass against us." The difference results from changes in the meanings of English words. At one time "debts" and "trespasses" meant essentially the same thing, sins or offenses against another person, and the words were interchangeable. Modern versions often translate the term more pointedly (and accurately) as "sins."

The Lord's Prayer is a model of how we should approach God in prayer. (The following text, found on the inside cover of *The Worshipbook* is used by many congregations.)

Our Father . . .	Establishes the intimacy of relationship.
who art in heaven . . .	Reminds us that God is transcendent too.
hallowed be thy name.	Brings us to worship God.
Thy kingdom come . . .	Articulates our longing for God's rule.
thy will be done on earth as it is in heaven.	Affirms that the basis of prayer is to be in tune with what God wants for us all.
Give us this day our daily bread;	Reminds us that our most basic needs are supplied by God alone.
Forgive us our debts	Makes forgiveness from God dependent on our
as we forgive our debtors;	ability to forgive others.
and lead us not into temptation, but deliver us from evil.	Appeals for the guidance and protection of God throughout life.
For thine is the kingdom, and the power, and the glory, forever.	A concluding act of praise to Almighty God.

(*See also* Daily Prayer; Prayer; Service for the Lord's Day.)

Lord's Supper.

The Lord's Supper and baptism are the two sacraments observed by most Protestant churches because they were commanded by Jesus (see Matt. 26:26–29; Mark 14:22–25; Luke 22:14–23; 1 Cor. 11:23–25; and Matt. 28:19–20). The Reformers of the sixteenth century understood the proper administration of the sacraments to be one mark of the true church, the other being the right proclamation of the Word.

The Lord's Supper sometimes goes by other names. *Communion* (or "Holy Communion") refers to our intimacy with God in sharing the elements and our fellowship with one another around the table. *Eucharist* (from the Greek for "thanksgiving") refers to the joy of the celebration. *The Breaking of Bread* is yet another name for the Lord's Supper.

From the beginning, the Lord's Supper was celebrated regularly. The people brought their bread and wine from home to share at the Lord's Table. Scripture was read and the gospel proclaimed, giving meaning to the actions of the Lord's Supper.

The connection between Word and sacrament was made early on and stressed by Calvin and other Reformers. Preaching presents the Word of God in Jesus Christ, the same person who is really present in the breaking of bread and the sharing of wine. Scripture and sermon prepare us for the sacrament, while the sacrament completes the proclamation of the Word. Christ is most fully revealed when both Word and sacrament are experienced (see Luke 24:13–32).

Whenever the Lord's Supper is shared, even in a sick room, scripture is to be read and briefly expounded. There should be no sacrament without scripture and sermon. Calvin and others also believed that the exposition of scripture without the Lord's Supper was also inadequate because the verbal proclamation of the Word was insufficient without the tangible experience of the Word through sharing the physical elements. It is thus appropriate to celebrate the Lord's Supper every Sunday, as is done in many Christian churches.

The elements of bread and wine (or grape juice) are common elements. There is nothing special or magical about them. What makes them special is that people recognize in them the self-giving love of God in Jesus Christ. In the acts of breaking bread, pouring wine, and sharing, Christ is present.

In the Reformed tradition, the elders serve the people so that those who govern may remember their role is that of servant, and the people are aware of receiving the Lord's Supper as a gift. When people serve one another in the pews, sharing the elements is a reminder of the people's mutual service in Christ. Even when the people come forward, their action is in response to the invitation of Christ, and they come not to take but to receive what Christ alone gives.

The Lord's Supper is related to the offering. The Reformers rejected a medieval notion that the sacrament represented a continual or repetitive sacrifice necessary for salvation, a concept not present in the early church. Jesus was the one who offered himself as a sacrifice before God (see Heb. 10:11–14). The bread and wine offered in the sacrament point to the sacrifice of Jesus Christ. Often the bread and wine are brought in procession with the offerings of the people. Care must be given to make clear that the bread and wine represent Christ's sacrifice and not ours, and that what we give is in response to God's self-giving action in Jesus Christ.

Transubstantiation (the idea that bread and wine actually change into the flesh and blood of Christ) was rejected by the Reformers. The idea never occurred to the early church but was a development of scholastic thought in the Middle Ages. Furthermore, the medieval mentality that produced such a thought is far from modern ways of thinking. The sacrament should not be seen as a magical act or an attempt to manipulate God.

The Reformers asserted a doctrine of "the real presence" of Christ in the Lord's Supper. Calvin, for example, saw the Lord's Supper not as a memorial meal recalling past events in which bread and wine are symbols of Christ's body and blood but as a meal at which the risen Christ is host, a meal in which we participate and encounter Christ now, in person.

The Great Prayer of Thanksgiving in the Lord's Supper is the supreme prayer of Christian worship where worshipers engage in prayer with God at the crux of their faith. In this prayer the full history of God's salvation is rehearsed, remembering that God has always had the redemption of God's people in mind, and in Jesus Christ this redemption was accomplished. Participating in the Lord's Supper, worshipers become participants in the history of God's salvation. What happened long ago becomes present now, just as the risen Christ is present in the sacrament to redeem God's people. (*See also* Acclamation; Agape Meal; Baptism; Bread/Wine; Chalice and Plate; Great Prayer of Thanksgiving; Institution, Words of; Offering; Preaching/Proclaiming the Word; Procession; Renewal of Baptism; Resurrection; Sacrament; Salvation History.)

Love Feast.

See Agape Meal.

Magnificat.

See Canticle.

Marriage.

Marriage began as primarily a contractual arrangement between a man and a woman. The early church often blessed such marriages but did not see them as essentially liturgical acts. Not until the Middle Ages did marriage enter the church liturgically. When social convention failed, the church filled the vacuum by providing liturgical means by which a man and a woman could be married. Even so, it took place on the front steps of the church, and the couple came into the church only if the Mass was to be celebrated. The medieval church began to think of marriage in sacramental terms in order to encourage it among the people because it was being neglected by civil authorities. The Roman Catholic Church declared marriage a sacrament at the Council of Trent (1546). The Reformers saw no need for marriage to be a sacrament but did provide orders for weddings in the church, primarily as the church's blessing of the relationship.

There are essentially three parts to a marriage: the betrothal, the vows, and the blessing. These are clearly recognizable today in wedding ceremonies. At first *the betrothal* took place at a time apart from the actual wedding, but in time significant parts of the betrothal were joined to the wedding itself. The advance notice aspect of the betrothal remained separate in the posting of the banns and is separate today in the announcement of engagements. The giving of a ring to the woman, originally signifying that she would be in charge of household goods, was part of the betrothal. Now rings are often exchanged within the marriage ceremony proper, signifying the sharing of life in all its aspects. The statements of intent at betrothal are today usually included in the wedding ceremony.

The exchange of vows is the act of marriage. The giving and receiving of rings is a tangible expression of the vows themselves. The couple then prays with the community for grace and strength to fulfill the vows made.

The third part of the service is *the blessing of the marriage*, its confirmation by the representative of the church, the minister. This is usually a brief statement that the couple is married, along with the pronouncement of God's blessing on them.

In this country, the minister who presides at a wedding is not only a representative of the church but of the state as well. The minister may not legally perform a wedding that has not been approved in advance by the state, with confirming documents presented by the couple. The minister is required by law to complete these forms for the state. The civil aspects of the marriage are legally binding, and in pronouncing the couple married, the minister serves as a functionary of the state. The religious and liturgical aspects are optional as far as the state is concerned.

In Calvin's practice, weddings were a part of the Sunday church service, taking place before the sermon. In Scotland weddings were prohibited on Sunday in deference to the holiness of the day. It is appropriate and possible today to have weddings as part of Lord's Day worship. A couple wanting their marriage to be firmly in the context of the community of faith might welcome this opportunity.

A wedding ceremony in the church is an act of worshiping God. As in all Christian worship, God is the focal point. The joyous celebration of a marriage goes beyond the romantic love of the two people to rejoice in God's gift of love in all relationships. The love of the couple is a reflection of God's love, which is the greater cause for rejoicing. Music and readings that extol human romantic love as the ideal have the effect of diminishing the wedding's impact as worship. All aspects of the wedding ceremony should point to God's redemptive love in Jesus Christ. (*See also* Music; Ordinances; Service for the Lord's Day.)

Maundy Thursday.

The name *Maundy* is applied to this day from the Latin word for "commandment" (from which we also get our word "mandate"). It refers to the commandment given by Jesus at the Last Supper that his disciples should love one another (see John 13:31–35).

The day has come to be one of the most important days of the Christian year in that it rehearses the events leading up to the crucifixion. It has a complex history, but the essentials are clear in the scriptural accounts and point to the meaning of God's redemptive act in Jesus Christ.

The service begins with a time for penitence, carrying on the theme of the season of Lent. The reading of scripture and a sermon may focus on the teachings of Jesus recorded in the Gospel of John (especially chapters 14 through 17). Footwashing may be included at this point in the service, emulating the acts of Jesus in washing his disciples' feet (John 13:1–20). Footwashing, however, is not a common modern practice, so its liturgical significance may not be readily apparent. Nevertheless, it is practiced liturgically by many Christians. The sacrament of the Lord's Supper is celebrated next, with its obvious connection to the Last Supper in the context of the Jewish Passover. Sometimes the service will conclude with

Tenebrae (from the Latin word for "shadows") where the rest of the story leading up to the crucifixion is rehearsed as candles are extinguished and darkness increases. Following the service, or as part of it, the place of worship may be stripped of all decorations and colors in anticipation of Good Friday.

Maundy Thursday is a time for focusing one's Lenten reflections on the mystery of redemption in the suffering and death of Jesus Christ. It is not a time to attempt to recreate the events in the Upper Room realistically, which would make the experience one of curiosity rather than of participatory faith. Rather, worshipers enter into the experience of Christ's death and resurrection in order to die with him and be raised to new life with him. (*See also* Good Friday; Lent; Lord's Supper; Tenebrae; Triduum.)

Meditation.

Meditation is the art of concentrating thoughtfully and prayerfully on a biblical text or theme. Worship may be considered comprehensively as an act of meditation on God. Some parts of worship are more inclined to be meditative, particularly instrumental or vocal music and the reading and hearing of scripture. Silences in worship are significant if they are used as opportunities for meditation. A congregation may be guided in meditation on a theme or even a passage of scripture by a worship leader.

A brief sermon is sometimes called a "meditation," but the term is inaccurate. Sermons are qualitatively different from meditations. One may meditate in the process of preparing a sermon, but one does not preach a "meditation." Perhaps one may share a meditation by verbalizing the product of personal reflection. This is very different from preaching, which is the proclamation of God's Word spoken in Jesus Christ. (*See also* Music; Preaching/Proclaiming the Word; Silence; Worship.)

Minister.

Specifically, the word is shorthand for "minister of Word and sacrament," a title given ordained clergy. The minister is the one who preaches and presides at the sacraments. Thus, the term applies particularly to the liturgical responsibilities of the clergy. Generally, the word may be accurately applied to any Christian, for all are "ministers," that is "servants" of Christ. (*See also* Benediction; Pastor; Preaching/Proclaiming the Word; Sacrament.)

Mission.

Mission is the reason for the existence of the people of God; they are to be God's agents to serve the rest of the world in the name of Jesus Christ. The people of God are called to go into the world. The mission of the church flows directly from its worship. What happens when the church is at worship affects how the church carries out its mission. Christian worship has a centrifugal force to it that pushes people out to be God's agents, by the power of Holy Spirit, with the risen Christ in the world. The people are gathered in order to be scattered.

The church scattered for mission is no less the church than when it is gathered for worship. The scattered church is empowered and unified by God's Holy Spirit, it encounters the risen Christ, and it serves God with justice and truth.

The mission of the church is global. Awareness of this fact enables Christians to work ecumenically. The mission thrust that sends us out of our worship into the world demands that we work with other Christians across denominational lines and beyond national interests.

The proclamation of the gospel includes an exhortation to mission. The Word of God present in Jesus Christ, addresses each worshiper and sends each one forth to fulfill a unique and personal mission as a disciple of Christ. Lives are claimed for this purpose as the gospel is announced as both challenge and empowerment.

The sacrament of baptism is the Christian's basic ordination to engage in mission work with Christ. This is the beginning of one's mission with other Christians.

The sacrament of the Lord's Supper is continual nurture

for people on God's mission in the world. It is bread for the journey of faith and drink that seals the covenant binding us to God in Jesus Christ and to one another in common ministry.

The charge is a deliberate sending forth of God's people, in the words of scripture, to be God's agents in the world. The benediction is the pronouncement and announcement of God's blessing of power on the people to complete their mission successfully.

There is a delightful ambiguity in the words "worship" and "service." They are, in many ways, interchangeable. There is, on the one hand, a service of worship and, on the other, the worship of service. We worship God in a worship service, and we go out to worship God with our service. The mission of the church is to go forth, tell, and do the gospel. It is in action that worship is proven authentic. (*See also* Baptism; Benediction; Ecumenism; Pew; Preaching/Proclaiming the Word.)

Music.

Music in worship serves the people by enabling them to worship God as more complete people. Words alone tend to be an intellectual exercise. Music touches a more subjective level and exercises the emotions. The combination of music and significant lyrical content involves the worshiper more completely than either one separately.

Even when music is played without lyrics being sung, the music may have theological content. Hymns that are played instrumentally will, of course, evoke thoughts of the hymn text, and the worshiper will be involved both intellectually and emotionally. More than that, however, music can carry thoughts and feelings that defy articulation. Music has the power to move and motivate people in intimate and personal ways.

In the worship of God, music enhances the message of the gospel, supporting praise, proclamation, and prayer. Hymns and anthems may be offered as articulations of the soul's deepest praise to Almighty God. There are also musical expressions that proclaim the Good News. Still other music gives wings to the prayers of the people. (*See also* Anthem; Hymn; Musician; Song; Spirituals.)

Musician.

A musician has a particular ministry in the life of the church. For all that music means and can mean in worship, the contribution of the musician is invaluable. The musician has God-given gifts and talents that are offered to God in the musician's own worship as well as shared with the community of faith as a ministry and service.

Often churches employ trained musicians to assure the carrying out of this ministry. There are amateur musicians as well in any congregation who may also make significant contributions to the worship of the whole church. One of the functions of the professional musician is to engage amateurs and enable them to contribute effectively to the worship experience.

The musician and the pastor work closely together because the purpose of music is to enhance the Word proclaimed in sermon and sacrament as well as to facilitate the people's expression of prayer and praise. Music is not an end in itself but an aid to the full worship of the whole people of God.

The musician—choir director or instrumentalist—will be astute in enabling the congregation as a whole to worship God, either by singing or in contemplation. The musician should avoid a "performance mentality," in the sense of performing for the entertainment of the worshipers. The musician will remember that he or she is a worshiper also, offering to God special gifts, leading all the people in the offering of their gifts of praise.

At times a musician will fill the role of "cantor," one who sings a text responsively with the congregation. The chanting of psalms or canticles is often done by a solo singer, who in turn leads the congregation in refrains. Other liturgical texts may also be sung by cantor and congregation in dialogue form. Worshipers are not there to be passive but to participate, and the cantor has much to contribute toward congregational involvement. (*See also* Antiphon; Choir; Music.)

Narthex.

This word is an architectural term that may or may not technically apply to a given church building. The narthex is a porch or vestibule that leads directly into the main part of the church, the nave. Whether or not your church has such a vestibule, the term is appropriately applied to any space that is used for people to wait as they are entering worship.

Since this is a place where people prepare for worship, it is important to consider what the narthex looks like to those entering. The decorations, symbols, bulletin boards, and the like give an impression that conditions the worshipers' approach to worship. If the narthex has the appearance of a lobby in a theater, for example, then the people's expectation will be to enter and watch a performance. The narthex can be a helpful introduction to the service. Liturgical colors may be used to denote the season and other decorations or visual symbols may be used to note a special day so that worshipers enter the worship space ready to worship.

As worshipers leave, the narthex is experienced from the opposite direction, and visual impressions will be different. Bulletin boards of community or church events can be placed to face exiting worshipers. Other symbols may be used so the narthex communicates a message of sending, as worshipers go into the world to be servants of Christ. (*See also* Colors; Congregation; Decorations; Mission; Nave; Symbols.)

Nave.

The *nave* of a church is that part of the worship space in which the congregation is located, usually the main part of the church. It comes from a Latin word meaning "ship" (as in our word "navy") and is derived from an ancient symbol for the church. The World Council of Churches' logo is a ship for this reason.

The analogy between a ship and the church building was drawn as early as the fourth century. The pews might be thought of as "rowers' benches," indicating the power of the people needed in the church. However, the church-ship is always pictured with a sail to suggest that the wind of God's Spirit propels it. The ship is always sailing on a mission for God and directed by the Word proclaimed in accord with the "chart" of scripture.

The placement of the pews in the nave can help the people focus on the center of worship. In earlier times, there were no pews or even chairs for the people, and the space of the nave was more flexible than in our day. Arrangement of the people's places may be varied, however, to make possible drama and dance, as well as alternate means of sharing in the Lord's Supper. (*See also* Choir; Congregation; Holy Spirit; Mission; Pew.)

Nicene Creed.

See Creed; Confession of Faith.

Nunc Dimittis.

See Canticle.

O Antiphons.

The *O Antiphons* are a set of seven ancient texts, each of which begins with the word "O" and addresses Christ by a title from the Old Testament:

> "O Wisdom. . . . " (Prov. 8:12)
> "O Adonai. . . . " (Exod. 20:2)
> "O Root of Jesse. . . . "(Isa. 11:1, 10)
> "O Key of David. . . . " (Isa. 22:22)
> "O Radiant Dawn. . . . "(Mal. 4:2; see also Luke 1:78)
> "O Ruler of the Nations. . . . " (Jer. 10:7)
> "O Immanuel. . . . " (Isa. 7:14)

They are in the form of sung prayers to the Messiah and follow a distinctive pattern. Each prayer attributes a quality to Christ consistent with the title and anticipating the petition. Each prayer bids Christ to come and fulfill the role inherent in the biblical title.

The first antiphon, for example, is:

> O Wisdom,
> coming forth from the mouth of the Most High,
> pervading and permeating all creation,
> you order all things with strength and gentleness:
> come now and teach us the way of salvation.

The O Antiphons are traditionally used during the seven days preceding Christmas Eve (December 17–23) at Evening Prayer, one on each day. They were originally used in this fashion, sung with the Song of Mary, the Magnificat. They may also be used on the Sunday before Christmas Eve (the Fourth Sunday of Advent) when all seven might be incorporated into the service. The O Antiphons express the longing of God's people for the promised Savior and are strong cries of petition for the Messiah to come. They can make a powerful contribution to the worship of the Advent season.

"O Come, O Come, Emmanuel" is a familiar hymn derived from some of the O Antiphons traditionally used during Advent. The term *antiphon* suggests that they were originally sung, perhaps in antiphonal (literally "voice against voice") style, as this hymn was originally. (*See also* Advent; Antiphon.)

Offering.

The offering of money during worship has long been associated with the Lord's Supper. One can imagine, from what we know, that what happened in the early church was something like this: The people brought bread and wine from their kitchen tables for sharing at the Lord's Table. The deacons saw to it that all the people were served, and when there was food left over, they took it to the poor. As people found out this was happening, they began to bring extra bread and wine to assure there would be plenty for distribution beyond the gathered congregation. As they recognized other needs around them, people would give the deacons money to buy clothing or whatever. As time went on, this all became institutionalized as part of the responsibilities of deacons. Even today there are churches where the deacons count the offering money and see that it is properly distributed.

Primarily the offering is a symbolic act signifying the worshipers' response to the Word of God. It is not so much an offering of money as it is the offering of oneself, which is the only reasonable offering (see Rom. 12:1). Money given is only a down payment on one's actions, a personal commitment to God to live sacrificially for Christ in every regard, to risk and dare in discipleship.

The giving of money enables the mission of the church to take place beyond the reach of the local congregation, even around the world. It is a way that every worshiper fulfills Christ's commandment to go into all the world (Matt. 28:19). Money takes our ministry where we cannot go. The Reformers placed almsgiving at the end of the service. It was a response of commitment on the way out of the church as worshipers began their service in the world.

For some, the offering is merely a bit of necessary business, the "collection of dues," which has to be done to keep the church financially afloat. If this is all there is to an offering in church, we could certainly find more efficient ways to do it by some accepted accounting process, such as monthly billing. It is important, however, that the people's offering of money be a part of their worship, so that giving money is seen as an act of serving God.

The offering appears in the order of service following the proclamation of the Word in scripture and sermon, in response to the call of God to each and all of us to service. It might also follow the confession of faith, showing that we not only say what we believe but intend to act it out.

The people's offering should not be confused with the offering of God's Son on the cross. Our sacrifices cannot supplant Christ's sacrifice. Our giving is always a response to God's self-giving. Our offering makes no sense whatever apart from the offering of Jesus Christ on the cross. Surely we give what we have because Christ gave his very life for us.

If the elements of the Lord's Supper are brought forward during the service (this is sometimes called "the Offertory"), it is appropriate to have them brought separately from the monetary offerings. The Reformed style has the Table set from the beginning of the service so that the anticipation of the meal is before the people the whole time. Another alternative is to have the elements brought forward as part of the entrance procession at the beginning of the service. This keeps the offering of money distinct from the presentation of bread and wine for Communion.

The people's gifts of money may be brought forward during the service and presented with a prayer, in which the people respond in thanksgiving to God's love and commit themselves to self-giving love in the name of Jesus Christ, by the power of Holy Spirit. Then the offering may be taken to the rear or placed conveniently near the front for the duration of the service. This is better than placing them on the Communion Table, which may give the impression that the people's offerings are of the same magnitude as Christ's. (*See also* Bread/Wine; Deacons; Lord's Supper; Mission; Service for the Lord's Day.)

Offertory.

Technically, the offertory is the presentation of the elements of bread and wine to be used in the Lord's Supper. In many Protestant churches, the offertory is the title bestowed on an anthem or piece of music designed to accompany the offering of the people's gifts of money. The music has an important purpose to serve, more than to cover the commotion made in passing plates or baskets to receive contributions. Its purpose is to provide a musical emphasis to encourage the dedication and commitment of the lives of the worshipers. Anthems should be uplifting in a challenging sense, calling the people to service. Other musical selections will similarly be of a tone to move and motivate worshipers to act on their faith. (*See also* Anthem; Choir; Music; Offering.)

Oil.

Oil is used for anointing. Olive oil (native to the eastern Mediterranean region) is traditionally used. If that is not available, a vegetable oil is preferred.

Oil is particularly valuable in arid climates. Oil is applied to protect and serve as an emollient for the skin. In this sense it is highly desired for good health. In the cultures of the Near East, the use of oil in this way symbolizes not only good health but wealth as well. In ancient cultures oil was available only to the very wealthy and to royalty. Oil glistening on the face meant a healthy person of means.

Anointing with oil has long been a part of the ministry to the sick (see Mark 6:13 and James 5:14–15). It is not a substitute for medical care but a physical reminder of the redemptive and healing grace of Jesus Christ. It is a sign that Christ brings healing for the whole person.

Anointing with oil also accompanies baptism as a sign that the baptized person belongs to Christ (God's Anointed One). In this context, oil becomes a reminder of one's identification with the royal person of God's Son. (*See also* Anointing; Baptism; Pastoral Care; Service for Wholeness.)

Order of service.

See Bulletin; Service for the Lord's Day.

Ordinances.

Ordinances are services "ordained" or authoritatively commanded to be observed. Generally the term refers to all services that are prescribed for the church by ecclesiastical authority. In some traditions an ordinance is specifically ordained by God and may be used to denote the sacraments or a particular rite for celebrating the sacraments. In some Protestant groups, just the opposite is true; "ordinances" refer to weddings, funerals, ordinations, and other liturgical events to distinguish them from the sacraments of the Lord's Supper and baptism. (*See also* Confirmation; Funeral; Marriage; Ordination; Sacrament.)

Ordinary Time.

The periods from the Baptism of the Lord through the Transfiguration of the Lord and from Trinity Sunday through Christ the King Sunday are called *ordinary time.* The meaning of "ordinary" is a positive one. These Sundays are the ordinary Sundays that establish the norm for Christian worship. The Sundays of ordinary time are the foundation of the Christian year, the bedrock of the liturgical calendar. On them are built the special days and seasons that shape the liturgical pilgrimage of God's people.

These two periods are also significant times in the course of the Christian year as they provide transitions between the Christmas and Easter cycles. Christmas and Easter are not interruptions of the Christian year but depend on the ordinary times for basic emphases. Both periods offer important opportunities for personal and corporate enrichment of faith as they work out themes of the incarnation and resurrection.

The liturgical color for ordinary time is green, suggesting the growth of plants, symbolizing spiritual growth and maturing in the faith. (*See also* Christian Year; Easter; Lord's Day/Sunday/Sabbath.)

Ordination.

In the Reformed tradition, ordination is understood as setting a person apart for a particular function. Ordination is sometimes viewed as the conferring of status upon an individual, but this is not true for Reformed Protestants. Whatever status might be attached to ordination is due to the importance of the function to which one is ordained.

In their effort to restore something of the primitive Christian church, some Reformers looked to the Bible to discover what needed to be done without fail if the church was to be the church. They found three tasks.

One is the proclamation of the Word, the announcement to the world that God's love has spoken in the Word-become-flesh, Jesus Christ. This is linked to the administration of the sacraments, the claiming of God's promise to be present in baptism and the Lord's Supper. These are combined in the dual responsibilities of one office, that of the pastor. Implicit in this function is the responsibility for teaching. Teaching and preaching, while distinct, are linked. Some Reformed churches term the minister the "teaching elder" to distinguish the office from that of the "ruling elder" who governs.

The second essential responsibility is governance. Someone has to be in charge in the church, to provide orderliness in God's household. More than that, we understand that if left to our own resources, we humans would not rise above our own sinfulness. There need to be people, accountable to God, with responsibility to keep order and to give direction. This important task is assigned to those called "elders" or sometimes "ruling elders."

The third essential function in the church's life is that of service. If the church is to be faithful to its servant Lord, it must be a servant as well, a self-giving servant in the style of Jesus Christ. The graces of generosity and liberality are to be cultivated, as well as efforts toward justice. Those for whom the world does not care are to be the particular concern of the church. This vital task is assigned to those called "deacons."

Special gifts are required to accomplish these essential functions. Those recognized for their wisdom are called to govern. Those who have particular abilities in scholarship and speaking are called to preach and preside in worship. Those with special capacities for compassion and caring are called to serve. Even so, those gifts will be enhanced by study and preparation.

Ordination to these functional offices is neither exhaustive nor exclusive. These three functions do not exhaust the many tasks to be performed in the life and mission of the church.

There are countless ministries carried out by all the people of the church, many of them seemingly small but all of them significant contributions to the whole enterprise. The three functions represented in ordinations are basic. Without them the church will not be faithful to God nor will it survive.

In the Reformed tradition, the functions carried out by ministers of Word and sacrament, elders and deacons, are not mutually exclusive. Ministers also engage in governance, but they are never in the majority, while elders are always in the majority on local church governing boards (sessions) and must at least have equal representation in other governing bodies. Elders can and should, from time to time, lead in worship. They are required, for example, to participate along with the clergy in administering the sacraments. Both ministers and elders take part in serving ministries even though deacons may lead the way.

The ordination of men and women to the ministry of Word and sacrament is done by the presbytery, which is the Reformed version of a bishop. While no ecclesiastical genealogy is kept, it is asserted that one ordained by the laying on of the hands of a presbytery, for example, is ordained in "apostolic succession." Thus, ordination is in the continuing tradition of the first apostles called by Jesus Christ. This is a reminder that the Word proclaimed in sermon and sacrament is Jesus Christ, who himself called the first apostles, and that the one ordained stands in that line.

Ordination to the ministry of Word and sacrament, to the office of elder, and to the office of deacon is essentially the same in Reformed churches. Identical questions are asked in each instance, with the exception of the one related to the office's particular function. Each ordination is to be held in honor, and every officer deserves the respectful support of the people. The service of ordination should always be a part of the worship of the whole congregation, for it is one of great significance for the life of the whole church of Jesus Christ. (*See also* Benediction; Deacons; Elder; Laying on of Hands; Minister.)

Organ.

The one musical instrument most closely associated with worship today is the organ. Many Christians find it difficult to imagine worship without the majestic strains of an organ.

The organ was mentioned as early as the third century in relationship to Christian worship. However, it was considered by many to be inappropriate for Christian worship and was resisted as a pagan instrument until the Middle Ages. Eastern Orthodox churches have never accepted the use of the organ or any other musical instruments. In the West, however, around the ninth century, the organ was introduced as an instrument that could bring harmony and richness to the music. Through the Middle Ages, the organ continued to develop, and it became increasingly involved in the liturgy. During the Renaissance, musical and technological advances contributed to the organ's popularity.

Protestant Reformers viewed the organ in basically two ways. For some, the organ was a symbol of the ornate and lavish Roman worship they were rejecting, so they not only did not use organs but even destroyed the ones they had. Others valued the organ as a wonderful instrument to accompany congregational singing. Presbyterian churches reinstalled organs in their churches in the nineteenth century.

The organ remains a vital part of Christian worship in many churches. It is certainly versatile, offering a rich array of sounds and musical possibilities on its own, and is suitable for accompaniment of solo, choral, or congregational singing.

Pipe organs are becoming increasingly expensive to build and to maintain, causing many churches to reassess their value. Fewer musicians are receiving training in organ, a fact that raises even more questions about the viability of an expensive organ in a church. Furthermore, electronic organs are rivalling pipe organs in tonal quality and capability at much lower costs.

The organ can provide a sense of continuity in a service

and certainly is a strong instrument to enhance a majestic sense of praising God. Its versatility is impressive, and its use as an instrument for accompanying singing can be inspiring. (*See also* Hymn; Music; Musician.)

Pall.

A pall is a cloth to be placed over a casket during a funeral service. It is usually white, symbolic of the resurrection, the white robes of the redeemed (Rev. 7:9), and baptismal garments. It is sometimes decorated with symbols of the resurrection such as the butterfly.

The purpose of the pall is to suggest that all are equal in the church. Since under the pall an expensive casket looks the same as a modest one, the use of a pall tends to discourage ostentation in funerals.

The pall is usually placed on the casket at the beginning of the funeral service, either before the procession or as it begins. Biblical texts are read as a reminder of the person's baptism (see Gal. 3:27 and Rom. 6:3–5). The body of the deceased may then be brought into the church, this last entrance recalling the person's first entrance into the church by baptism. (*See also* Baptism; Funeral; Procession.)

Palm Sunday.

Palm Sunday begins Holy Week with a liturgical dramatization of the triumphant entrance of Jesus into Jerusalem (see Matt. 21:1–11; Mark 11:1–11; Luke 19:28–40; and John 12:12–19).

The church's celebration of Palm Sunday dates from the late fourth century, and it originated in the Jerusalem church with a great afternoon procession from the Mount of Olives into the city. Children took part in the parade, and everyone carried palm branches.

Modern service books often connect Palm Sunday with a "Passion Sunday" emphasis. Palm Sunday is celebrated by a procession of palms at the beginning of the service. The celebration is muted, anticipating the subsequent events of Holy Week, which are proclaimed in the reading of the Passion narrative. The end of the service points like an arrow to the crucifixion.

The color for Palm Sunday is usually purple, as for the rest of Lent. Some churches use a dark red for all of Holy Week, beginning with Palm Sunday, to symbolize the blood of Christ on the cross. This latter color is more appropriate if there is a Passion Sunday emphasis. (*See also* Christian Year; Holy Week; Passion Sunday; Procession.)

Pascha.

Pascha is a transliteration of the Hebrew word for Passover and refers to that event (see Exodus 12). The Christian church adopted the term to refer to the crucifixion and resurrection of Jesus Christ, the Christian Passover. Most often it is used as an adjective. The Paschal candle, for example, is the large candle lighted at the Paschal Vigil, the service on the eve of Easter. (*See also* Easter Vigil, Paschal Candle.)

Paschal Candle.

The Paschal candle is lighted at the beginning of the Easter Vigil from a new fire symbolizing the victory of the resurrection of Christ over the darkness of death. The candle is a large one, often specially made for this purpose. It may be inscribed with a cross, the Greek letters alpha and omega, and the current year's date. Sometimes five grains of incense are inserted into the candle, signifying the wounds of Christ on the cross. A new candle is usually secured for each Easter Vigil. In addition to its use during the Easter Vigil, the candle is kept lighted throughout the Easter season. It may also be used at other times during the year.

When a candle is given at a baptism, it can be lighted from the Paschal candle, which may be located near the font and lighted for the occasion (unless it is during the season of Easter and the candle is already burning).

The Paschal candle may also be used as part of the procession for a funeral, following the processional cross and then placed at the head of the coffin. (*See also* Baptism; Easter Vigil; Funeral; Procession.)

Passion Sunday.

Passion Sunday was traditionally observed the fifth Sunday in Lent (the week before Palm Sunday) because the Gospel reading for that day told of the crucifixion. In modern times, some have found it confusing to recall the crucifixion, then a week later remember the triumphal entry into Jerusalem, and on Good Friday return to the crucifixion.

Hence, Passion Sunday has been attached to Palm Sunday, now referred to as "Passion/Palm Sunday" (also called in some churches "Palm/Passion Sunday"). Actually, this is an echo of an ancient arrangement dating from the fourth century.

The Passion/Palm Sunday combination is a concession to the fact that today few worshipers attend weekday services, even during Holy Week. To go from the Palm Sunday celebration directly to the Easter celebration bypasses the necessary emphasis on the crucifixion. The full pilgrimage through Holy Week can be the most profound liturgical experience of the year, and to telescope the Passion into a part of a Sunday service may diminish its importance. In either event, it is necessary that the crucifixion of Christ be approached in sober meditation so that the joy of Christ's resurrection may be profoundly appropriated.

The appropriate colors for this day are purple, as for the rest of Lent, or dark red. (*See also* Christian Year; Crucifixion; Holy Week; Lent; Palm Sunday.)

Pastor.

The pastor of a congregation has responsibilities far beyond the liturgical ones. However, all pastoral functions are directly related to the worship experience.

The pastor of a congregation guides the people to God. The pastoral role is essential in the leadership of worship, for with caring and sensitivity the pastor, elders, and others responsible for worship lead the people in their praise and personal commitments before God.

The term "pastor" may be distinguished from "minister." A pastor is the servant leader of the people as they come before God, while a minister of Word and sacrament is primarily the servant of God to the people.

While the pastor often relates one-on-one with people, the corporate experience of worship is a reminder that the pastor is to be the shepherd of the whole flock. The universality of human need and sinfulness is brought home in the corporate experience of worship. The community is made up of people being pastors to one another, which is also evident in the worship experience.

The pastor stands in the tradition of the rabbi and as the liturgical representative of Christ certainly has this role. The pastor is a teacher and should be involved in the educational process of the congregation at all age levels. This teaching role is related to, but not precisely the same as, the pastoral responsibility as minister of the Word, the expositor of scripture in preaching. As a student of scripture, the pastor will find teaching a learning and growing experience necessary to the fulfillment of other pastoral responsibilities.

Baptism and the Lord's Supper provide pastoral opportunities as well. In preparatory counseling for baptism the pastor (and other leaders) engage with families in the upbringing of children and with adults in their own spiritual nurture. The Lord's Supper is the continuing sacrament that calls us to nurturing relationships with the risen Christ and with each other. Pastoral situations of grief and sorrow, of birth and death, of anxiety and despair find a focus in the sacraments, and the one who presides liturgically is the same one who ministers pastorally. (*See also* Baptism; Lesson; Lord's Supper; Minister; Ordination; Pastoral Care; Preaching/Proclaiming the Word.)

Pastoral Care.

The service for the Lord's Day offers a number of opportunities for expressions of *pastoral care*, that is, for the minister of Word and sacrament to lead the people in worship with sensitivity to their human needs.

If the service of worship is to be truly "liturgy," the work of the people, then the leader of worship must see to it that all are drawn into participation. The service generally should not display exclusivity that would leave any out of the worship experience. Language, for example, should always be inclusive.

The prayer of confession is a liturgical form of what often happens in private pastoral conversations and counseling. The same sensitivity is required here; forgiveness rather than judgmental attitudes should be conveyed.

In the sermon, the pastor-preacher should recognize that the preacher him- or herself is first a listener. A pastoral sensitivity to the human condition should be evident. The preacher should hold up for all, preacher included, the potential for Christlike living and claim with the people God's promises of power for new life in Jesus Christ. The call of God and challenge to the people should be accepted by the preacher as well.

Announcements are usually printed and made orally during the service. These also can display the caring of the whole community for all its members and for those beyond it.

Intercessory prayers, of course, have the most obvious pastoral content. Here the needs of those in the congregation and those around it are held up to God for God's grace, mercy, and wholeness.

The sacraments are opportunities as well to enact liturgically the pastoral nurture of the church, making a commitment thereby to carry it out in the church's program. (*See also* Announcements; Baptism; Confession of Sin; Intercession; Language of Worship; Liturgy; Minister; Pastor; Preaching/Proclaiming the Word.)

Peace (Greeting of).

The Greeting of Peace (or the "Kiss of Peace") is one of the oldest aspects of Christian worship. Jesus taught that one should not come before God unreconciled with one's neighbor (see Matt. 5:23–24). This teaching was remembered and ritualized in Christian worship at an early date. Paul admonished his readers to greet one another with a holy kiss (see Rom. 16:16); 1 Cor. 16:20; 2 Cor. 13:12; 1 Thess. 5:26) and Peter gave similar instructions (see 1 Peter 5:14).

The Greeting of Peace has been revived in the worship services of many churches, taking basically two different forms. In some situations it is done very informally. People simply greet one another with a handshake or hug. In other places it is more formalized with the greeting scripted in liturgical words for worshipers to say to one another, such as, "The peace of Christ be with you," or simply, "Peace be with you," to which the other responds, "And also with you."

While an informal greeting may have value as a personal greeting, it may also be nothing more than that. The problem with this kind of informality is that it tends to discount the deeper meaning of the ritual, namely that the "peace of Christ" we share is not our own; it is Christ who reconciles us to one another and gives us peace.

The more formal and ritualized greeting has value in that it emphasizes the peace of Jesus Christ as the content of our greeting, setting it above the mundane. The problem is that this, too, can become ritualized in the worst sense of the word and become for many a meaningless act.

However it is done, the Greeting of Peace should emphasize the peace of Christ in which we live together in the church. The peace of Christ, which we receive as a gift of grace, makes it possible for us to be at peace with one another.

The location of the Greeting of Peace in the order of service is important. If it is done at the very beginning of the service, it may be difficult to understand it as anything more than the mundane greeting among people. Its traditional location is between the proclamation of the Word in scripture and sermon, and the Lord's Supper. Having heard God's Word and its inherent pronouncement of peace, we practice that peace immediately as preparation to come to the Table. The liturgical ritual of the Greeting of Peace then becomes a commitment on each worshiper's part to seek the peace of Christ in all relationships in and beyond the community of faith. (*See also* Lord's Supper; Service for the Lord's Day.)

Pentecost.

The Day of Pentecost marks the end of the Easter season. The word *Pentecost*, taken from the Greek, means "fifty days," and the festival is derived from the Jewish festival of Shavuot, which took place fifty days after Passover. The Jewish festival was an annual commemoration of the giving of the Law to Moses and the establishment of a new relationship between Israel and God. Pentecost indicates the establishment of a new relationship between God and the new Israel, the followers of Jesus Christ.

Pentecost is the celebration of the creation of the church of Jesus Christ as recorded in Acts 2. As Christ was raised from the dead, the Body of Christ was given new life by the Spirit (breath) of God. This is the church's spiritual birthday.

The life-giving Spirit sends the church into the world to carry out Christ's mission. The church is clearly a world church, proclaiming the Word of God in Jesus Christ to all peoples. Babel (Gen. 11:1–9) is undone as the message is heard in every tongue (Acts 2:5–11). The church goes forth into all the world, breaking down walls and overcoming divisions that keep people from knowing their true unity in God.

Red is the traditional color, suggesting the fire of the Spirit coming on the church at Pentecost. (*See also* Christian Year; Ecumenism; Holy Spirit; Mission.)

Petition.

Petition is a form of prayer that asks God directly for what we want. The difficulty comes when what we want is not what we need. Nevertheless, our prayers of petition help us articulate our deepest wants and longings. Knowing that God is aware of our needs, the encounter of prayer becomes a dialogue in which we are made aware of our needs as well and sensitive to the presence of God in our lives meeting those needs.

We do not change God's mind by our prayers; rather we are changed. The bottom line in every Christian prayer is from the model our Lord gave us, "Thy will be done" (Matt. 6:10), as seen also in his example in the Garden of Gethsemane (see Matt. 26:39). Yet we ask, and ask again, for we are to be persistent in prayer (see Luke 11:5–13). (*See also* Intercession; Prayer; Worship.)

Pew.

For centuries there were no seats in church naves. The worshipers stood throughout the worship service, as is the custom even today in many Eastern Orthodox churches. In the Middle Ages elaborately carved pews were introduced in Europe, but only after the Reformation did pews became common. Pews in Reformed churches were plain and undecorated, often with high backs and sides that kept drafts away, but also had the effect of isolating worshipers from one another.

Pews have a symbolic significance. In keeping with the image of the church as a ship, the pews may be thought of as the "rowers' benches"; the people provide some of the power to move the church on its mission. Of course, God's breath (Holy Spirit) blows the church-ship on its way, but the people participate with God in making the mission happen.

In colonial America, and even down to recent times, pews have been "rented" or "sold" as a way of raising funds for the local church as well as guaranteeing members regular seats. This practice was abandoned in the nineteenth century because it tends to encourage a status consciousness inappropriate to Christian worship.

Many feel that pews have an inhibiting effect on worship

and contribute to congregational passivity. In many churches the placement of the pews is permanent and can be limiting. Pitched floors also prevent any change in arrangement. Stackable chairs may provide the most flexible possibilities for liturgical arrangements, but their use requires a flat floor. (*See also* Congregation; Mission; Nave.)

Postlude.

The postlude is musical accompaniment to the exit dance of the people. It is not a performance of music for its own sake but serves the purpose of encouraging the going forth of the people into the world to be Christ's servants and witnesses. Sometimes the postlude will encourage a reflective moment as worshipers contemplate the implications of the charge and benediction, their mission for Christ, and the gift of empowerment. The postlude is a musical enhancement of the scattering of the church into the world in service (diakonia). (*See also* Benediction; Dance; Diakonia; Mission; Recessional.)

Posture.

See Gesture and Posture.

Praise.

All worship is fundamentally praise and always begins there. Underlying all of worship is a sense of adoration of God in response to God's mighty acts of salvation.

While praise may be considered a particular kind of prayer, it is also the basis for prayer. We cannot confess unless we have praised God and recognized God's greatness alongside our own small stature. We cannot petition God or intercede for others unless we have praised God who is the Almighty One who can accomplish that for which we pray. We give thanks only when we have praised God as the One from whom all blessings flow. We will dedicate ourselves to God insofar as we have praised God as worthy of our devotion.

Praise may pour forth without words on the wings of song and music, lifting to God the joy of the soul (see Rom. 11:33–36). (*See also* God; Music; Prayer; Worship.)

Prayer.

Prayer is our encounter with God as God's own people and may include our words, thoughts, meditations, contemplations, and receptive silences. Prayer is usually understood, more narrowly, as a conscious act of focusing on God, of encountering God, and finding words to express one's faith and need.

There is a useful acronym that serves as a reminder and summary of the kinds of prayer: *ACTIP*, standing for adoration, confession, thanksgiving, intercession, and petition. All our prayers fall into one or another of those categories.

The sequence is instructive as well. We begin with *adoration*, praising God for being God, standing in joyful wonder and awe at God's greatness. Then we are moved to *confession*, for if we recognize God to be great, we quickly see our own smallness; if God is great and awe-inspiring, we are feeble and frail; if God is just and true, we are petty and judgmental; if God is holy, we are sinful. The gap between God and us is the abyss of sin. We are alienated from God, separated from who God wants us to be, isolated from one another. This we confess. God has already offered forgiveness and deliverance from sin's bondage by the redemptive act of Jesus Christ. To this we respond in *thanksgiving*. Having received this gift of freedom from sin's power and the promise of new life, we know God cares for all sinful people like ourselves, and we are moved to *intercessions*, praying for those around us. We are also bold, however, to make our own *petitions*, for we know our needs continue.

The Lord's Prayer models the various kinds of prayer. God is acknowledged to be holy (adoration); we ask for forgiveness (confession); we indicate our willingness to forgive others (intercession); we ask for daily bread and deliverance from evil (petition), and the whole prayer has overtones of thanksgiving.

In its first word, the Lord's Prayer reminds us that prayer is a corporate activity. One may pray alone in the solitude of one's room, but one's prayer rises up out of the community of God's people. God is the God of all of us, not just of each of us. The distinction made between corporate and private prayer is false if it assumes that only private prayer can be personal. Corporate prayer will be personal if it is fed by the discipline of daily prayer by the members of the body. In the other direction, private prayer will have the support of the whole community if it flows from the worship of the gathered body. We learn how to pray by praying together, by sharing the prayers of the church in worship, as well as by reading the scriptures and meditating on biblical prayers.

Through the centuries a controversy has persisted regarding the relative merit of written prayers as opposed to free prayer. Written prayers, whether they are composed by the worship leader in advance of the service or prayers from a denominational prayer book, are spurned by some because they seem to limit the free flow of the Spirit in prayer. Spontaneous prayer seems more open to the working of the Spirit in that moment. Advocates of written prayers, however, argue that classic prayers that have survived for years provide substantive examples for people who are groping for the words with which to pray. Surely, they suggest, the Spirit may work in and through the person writing down a prayer as well as in the moment during a worship experience. Furthermore, they cite Jesus as one who taught prayer by giving an example of how to pray, which we rehearse liturgically in the Lord's Prayer. It is also true that improvised prayer takes on a sameness after a while, with catch phrases and code words themselves becoming a set form.

The controversy is likely to continue, as it should. There is a healthy tension between freedom and form, for it is in that tension that the dynamic power of the Spirit comes into play. Classic prayers of the ages are instructive, and written prayers that are well thought out bring disciplines of study and meditation to corporate prayer. Yet worshipers and their leaders should cultivate the art of extemporaneous prayer to experience more fully a sense of personal involvement. Both approaches working together enable openness to the guidance of God's Spirit.

There are a number of biblical examples of prayer by which we might be led in developing our own prayers. Besides the Lord's Prayer, the following might also be noted:

The priestly prayer of Moses (Num. 14:13–19)
David's prayer of thanksgiving (1 Chron. 17:16–27)
Solomon's prayer at the dedication of the Temple (1 Kings 8:22–61)
Many Psalms, including especially
   Prayer of anguish and praise (Psalm 22)
   Prayer of confession (Psalm 51)
   Prayer for help (Psalm 130)
   Prayer of intimacy (Psalm 139)
Simeon's Song (Luke 2:28–32)
The Prayer of Jesus in Gethsemane (Matt. 26:36–44; also Mark 14:32–39; Luke 22:39–46)
The Priestly Prayer of Jesus (John 17:1–26)

(*See also* Collect; Confession of Sin; Great Prayer of Thanksgiving; Intercession; Lord's Prayer; Petition; Praise; Prayer for Illumination; Prayer of Thanksgiving; Prayer of the Day; Worship.)

Prayer for Illumination.

The Prayer for Illumination is offered immediately before the reading of scripture or before the sermon, praying that all may be enlightened by the biblical message. It is a prayer for the preacher as well as for the congregation, for the preacher is listener before being a speaker of God's Word. The prayer acknowledges that in the proclamation of the Word in scripture and sermon, God is speaking. Human words and voices are only agents by which God is heard.

The Prayer for Illumination further stresses that the Word is not only to be heard but to be obeyed, the listener's will is to be affected. Not simply understanding is sought but a pervasive enlightenment that will change the listener's life.

The use of this prayer is most common in Reformed churches although it is also used in other traditions. This is a typical prayer of illumination:

Prepare our hearts, O Lord, to accept your word. Silence in us any voice but your own; that, hearing, we may also obey your will; through Jesus Christ our Lord. Amen. (From *The Worshipbook*, p. 28.)

(*See also* Bible/Scripture/Word of God; Prayer; Prayer of the Day.)

Prayer of Thanksgiving (Prayer of Thanks).

The Prayer of Thanksgiving (or Prayer of Thanks) is used in place of the Great Prayer of Thanksgiving when the Lord's Supper is not celebrated. While shorter, it is similar in structure to the Great Prayer of Thanksgiving.

In this prayer all thanksgiving to God is rooted in the offering of thanks for the gift of God's Son to be the Savior of the world. The prayer may follow the offering of monetary gifts, but it will lead worshipers beyond being thankful merely for material blessings to a heartfelt thanksgiving for the blessings of new life in Jesus Christ.

The Prayer of Thanksgiving, like the Great Prayer of Thanksgiving, should reflect seasonal and special day emphases. (*See also* Christian Year; Great Prayer of Thanksgiving; Offering; Prayer.)

Prayer of the Day.

The Prayer of the Day encapsulates the theme or emphasis of the particular Lord's Day. It is often used at or near the beginning of a service for this reason, but it may also be used before the reading of scripture.

The Prayer of the Day usually asks God's direction and inspiration in the time of worship and is appropriately used as an opening prayer or to conclude the opening segment, coming before the scripture and sermon. Prayers of the day ordinarily take the form of a collect. (*See also* Christian Year; Collect; Prayer; Service for the Lord's Day.)

Preaching/Proclaiming the Word.

Preaching is one of two marks of the true church as identified by the reformers in the sixteenth century—the Word of God rightly proclaimed and the sacraments duly administered.

The proclamation of the Word of God is a central element in Christian worship. The Word proclaimed is none other than Jesus Christ, the Risen One, present to us in our worship. Christ is the Word-made-flesh, God-with-us, the divine in human form, the One who died and is risen. Christ is the Word of God (see John 1:1–4, 10–14).

This Word is proclaimed in worship first through the reading of scripture. The Bible is positioned prominently to remind us of the centrality of God's Word revealed in the scripture. It is not the *words* of God that we find in the words of the Bible; rather it is the *Word*, namely Jesus Christ.

The sermon is based on the Bible. In some churches the preacher speaks from text or notes literally resting on the open Bible. Doing so reminds both preacher and people that the sermon is to be an exposition of scripture. That is, the sermon is to present to the congregation the living Christ, the Word revealed in scripture.

The sermon, then, is not the preacher's opinions but an announcement of God's good news in the death and resurrection of the Lord. The preacher is first a listener to God's Word. Long before uttering a word from the pulpit, the preacher engages the living Word in scripture and listens for God's voice speaking to these people in this time at this place. Most clergy have traditionally been trained to study the scripture using the resources of scholarship and the ability to read Hebrew and Greek, the original languages of the biblical texts.

The people in the pews similarly have a responsibility for

preaching. A sermon is not to be judged by whether or not one agrees with it. A sermon is to be an encounter of the listener with the living Lord, that Word of God revealed in scripture. Worshipers, then, must come to church prepared by study and prayer to hear the sermon and engage the Word (Christ). Sermons are often based on the Common Lectionary, a schedule of Bible readings for each Sunday. This makes it possible for worshipers to look ahead and anticipate God's message as proclaimed in scripture and sermon. (*See also* Bible/Scripture/Word of God; Kerygma; Lectern; Lectionary; Lesson; Minister; Pastor; Pulpit.)

Prelude.

The prelude is musical accompaniment to the entrance dance of the people. It is not a performance of music for its own sake but serves to announce the gathering of the people into the fellowship of faith to be nourished and strengthened as Christ's servants and witnesses. Sometimes the prelude encourages a reflective moment by the worshipers as they anticipate the time to be spent in worship of God in the presence of the living Christ. The prelude is a musical enhancement of the gathering of the church into Christian fellowship (koinonia). (*See also* Dance; Koinonia; Procession.)

Procession.

The entrance of the people of God into worship is dramatized by the procession of worship leaders, which may include clergy, choir, congregational leaders or officers, and lay readers. The procession may also include a cross and candles, signifying that we enter worship following the lead of our Lord Jesus Christ. At a funeral the casket may be brought in the procession after the pall is placed over it, recalling the baptism by which the deceased first entered the church.

The clergy may want to enter before the procession and take their places to prepare silently for the service, thus setting a visual example for the people in their preparations.

At certain times during the year processions assume a major role in worship. One is Palm Sunday, remembering the entry of Jesus into Jerusalem at the beginning of Holy Week. A procession on Good Friday may recall the "way of the cross," with a rough cross carried into the church or with readings and prayers before stations of the cross. At Easter Vigil there is also a procession as the Paschal candle is brought in, the people lighting their candles from it as they enter the darkened church. (*See also* Easter Vigil; Funeral; Good Friday; Pall; Palm Sunday.)

Profession of Faith.

See Confession of Faith.

Psalms.

Psalms are meant to be sung by the people. This use of the Psalms is a high form of worshiping God, in that God is praised in the very inspired words of scripture and the songs of the people are joined with those of the hosts of heaven. The Book of Psalms is, in fact, a collection of at least five "hymnals" used to sing God's praise in ancient Jewish worship.

Presbyterians and others have traditionally been known as "psalm-singers." They believe they are being true to scripture by singing the Psalms. Not to sing them in some fashion would be unbiblical and therefore inadequate worship.

The principal way the Psalms were sung by early Reformed groups was in metrical versions. This required retranslating the Psalms into hymnlike texts that had meter and rhyme. These became very popular and remain even today a great contribution to the musical praise of God. Examples found in most hymnals include Psalm 121, paraphrased as "I to the Hills Will Lift My Eyes," and Psalm 23 as "The Lord's My Shepherd." Metrical versions of the Psalms are sometimes difficult to distinguish from regular hymns since they often look and sound like hymns. The difference is that, although a hymn may be based on a scriptural text, it is a piece of poetry on its own, while a metrical psalm adheres more closely to the biblical text.

Another way of singing the Psalms came to American churches through the English and Scottish chanting traditions. In Protestant churches chanting is relatively simple when compared to chanting in the Roman, Anglican, or Orthodox traditions. It is a way of singing a prose text without the necessity of further translation and has the appeal of keeping the text unchanged from scripture reading. It allows more stress to be put on the words so their meaning is heightened. It has a musical quality that puts the praise of the Psalms into song. While chanting the Psalms may be new to many Protestants today, one has only to consult older denominational hymnals to discover many chants, not to mention the Church of Scotland's Psalter, which provides a number of ancient and traditional chants.

Sometimes psalms are said or sung "responsively" or "antiphonally," alternating verses or lines between the leader and the congregation. This method emphasizes the parallelism of the Hebrew poetry in the Psalms but does not always emphasize the meaning.

When a psalm is not sung in a metrical version or chanted but only read aloud, the people may join in singing a response, which is usually a phrase from the psalm itself. In this way at least a gesture is made in the direction of singing the psalm.

The psalm is usually sung as the congregation's musical response to the reading from the Old Testament (Hebrew Scriptures). In this way we praise God for the Word of God revealed in that text and stand with God's people Israel in our worship. Through the singing of the psalm we pray the psalm, making those words our own words, so that we praise God in the language of scripture. Singing reminds us that the Psalms are not mere human words but are inspired to help us go beyond ourselves to praise God. In this way we grow in praise and learn better how to pray.

For centuries the only singing done in Reformed churches was the Psalms. Psalters were developed so the people could sing in worship. This was essential, according to Calvin and others, in that singing engages the complete person in worship and provides a unity among worshipers. Calvin, in fact, recruited Louis Bourgeois (c. 1510–61) to compose singable tunes to which the Psalms could be sung. Many of these tunes remain today in modern hymnals.

For the Reformers the distinction between hymns and psalms sung in worship was that hymns were of human composition, while the Psalms had the divine stamp on them, coming as they did from Holy Writ. With the advent of great hymn writers such as Isaac Watts and the Wesleys, the distinction was blurred. Even Presbyterians published psalters and hymnals under one cover although there were separate sections. By the nineteenth century, psalms and hymns were sung interchangeably in most Protestant churches. (*See also* Antiphon; Chant; Hymn; Psalter; Service for the Lord's Day; Song.)

Psalter.

The Book of Psalms is sometimes called "the Psalter," but more often the term is used for a collection of psalms to be used in worship. Some psalms cannot be readily read aloud or sung. Therefore, a psalter may not contain the usual biblical text but a special translation designed to be sung, said, or heard. The result is more a paraphrase than a precise literal translation. Musical settings for the Psalms may be supplied so that a psalm can be sung in worship. Chants are commonly used to sing psalm texts although metrical renderings make hymn tunes useable as well as specially composed tunes.

In Lord's Day worship the Psalter selection is usually designated as a response to the reading from the Old Testament (Hebrew Scriptures). The people thus sing a response to the Old Testament passage, praising God in the words of the ancient prayer book and hymnal of God's people. The Psalter selection, therefore, may be a psalm or a portion of a psalm. Its function is not the same as the other readings in which scripture is read to be heard and obeyed. In the Psalter, the psalm is itself the response. Therefore some congregational participation in the Psalter by way of a response, spoken or sung, is almost mandatory.

The Common Lectionary includes a schedule of Psalms selected as responses to each Sunday's lesson from the Old Testament (Hebrew Scriptures). Many of these find expression in musical settings in many hymnals.

New psalters are available or are being developed by several denominations. Settings are provided for many if not all psalms, including chants, metrical versions, and anthemlike pieces, all of which give a tremendous variety to a congregation's expression in worship. (*See also* Bible/Scripture/Word of God; Chant; Lectionary; Psalms; Service for the Lord's Day.)

Pulpit.

The pulpit as we know it is a relatively recent innovation, coming into frequent use about the same time as seats were placed in the church nave (the late fifteenth century). In the early church, preaching was done by the bishop from a chair (*ex cathedra*) behind the Table, the seated position being considered appropriate for the teaching role (see Matt. 5:1).

In many churches the pulpit is on one side, leaving the Table in the center. Often the pulpit is balanced with a lectern on the other side from which the scripture lessons are read and the prayers led. This arrangement is called a "divided chancel." The pulpit is sometimes placed in the center, usually above and behind the Table, thus displaying the centrality of Word and sacrament in Reformed worship. For the sake of consistency, the font ought also to be centrally located, probably in front of the Table. With a central pulpit, the open Bible is often displayed on the pulpit, which is also the lectern for scripture reading, making clear that the sermon is intended to be an exposition of scripture.

Using the imagery of the church as ship, the pulpit may be thought of as the deck where the course is charted based on scripture. (*See also* Chancel; Font, Baptismal; Lectern; Nave; Preaching/Proclaiming the Word; Table.)

Reaffirmation of Baptismal Vows.

See Renewal of Baptism.

Reaffirmation of Faith.

See Confession of Faith; Confirmation.

Recessional.

The recessional is the exit of the choir, clergy, and other worship leaders at the end of the service, dramatizing the going forth of the people into the world to live for Christ. The clergy may wish to remain after the recessional hymn to give the charge and benediction face-to-face with the congregation rather than from behind them. Or the charge and benediction may be given before the recessional hymn that concludes the service. (*See also* Benediction; Mission; Postlude.)

Reformation Day.

Reformation Day is observed October 31, the day in 1517 on which Martin Luther nailed Ninety-five Theses for debate on the door of the Wittenberg Church and started the sequence of events that resulted in what is called the Protestant Reformation. On this day we remember with thanksgiving the grace of God that prompted that great reformation in the church and that continues to provide for its reform. Remembering the historical events of the sixteenth century, we confess our need for renewal and reformation in the church today.

This is an opportunity to celebrate some of the great themes of the Reformation, such as the priesthood of all believers, affirming the full participation of God's people in the life of the church.

Reformation Day may be recognized in Lord's Day worship the Sunday before October 31. (*See also* Christian Year; Hymn; Laity/Lay Reader/Lay Leader.)

Remembrance.

See Anamnesis.

Renewal of Baptism.

Baptism does not guarantee moral perfection. Whenever one is baptized, as an infant or as an adult, one continues to be a sinner. Baptism is the claim of God's promise of new life in Jesus Christ and the commitment to live as Christ's disciple. There is always room for spiritual growth.

The church has thus understood a need for occasions on which people can renew their baptisms. Some occasions are readily available. Every time people share in the Lord's Supper or participate in the baptism of another, they may renew their baptisms, claiming once again God's promises of love and recommitting themselves to Christ's service.

Many denominations provide special services for the renewal of baptism on a variety of occasions. At the time of confirmation, people who have been baptized as infants reaffirm the vows made at their baptisms. A congregation as a whole may renew baptism in the Easter Vigil if there are no baptisms to be celebrated. Other occasions in the life of a congregation, such as the installation or departure of a pastor, or significant anniversaries, may appropriately include the renewal of baptism. Ministry with the sick and dying often presents the opportunity for renewing baptismal vows. Pastoral care may warrant a private ceremony for the renewal of a person's baptism. Those commissioned to some special work in the church or called to a new ministry may welcome the opportunity for the renewal of baptism as their new service begins. When members are received by a congregation or reactivated, the renewal of baptism may be a powerful experience of worship.

It becomes clear in all of this that baptism is not the culmination of one's faith but the beginning of a faith-journey that continues through one's whole life. Renewal of baptism is like a series of signposts to be consulted frequently and at many points along the way to make sure that we are headed in Christ's direction. Baptism is to be experienced only once, but it is to be remembered many times. (*See also* Affirmation of Faith, Baptism; Baptism of the Lord; Confession of Faith; Confirmation; Cross, Sign of; Easter Vigil; Lord's Supper; Pastoral Care; Renunciation of Evil; Service of Wholeness.)

Renunciation of Evil.

At the time of baptism, the one being baptized, or parents or sponsors of that person, renounces evil while affirming faith in Jesus Christ.

In some Protestant churches the renunciation has not been explicit but considered implicit in the affirmation. When one turns toward Christ, one turns away from all that is not Christ; when one accepts Christ's lordship, one rejects the dominion of all in the world that opposes Christ. Many Protestants are today reclaiming the renunciation as an explicit part of the baptismal liturgy, as it is in Roman Catholic, Anglican, and Orthodox traditions. This is in recognition of the power of evil that would claim human loyalty. A clear rejection of evil reinforces one's affirmation of loyalty to Jesus Christ. (*See also* Affirmation of Faith; Baptism.)

Reproaches.

See Solemn Reproaches from the Cross.

Responses.

All worship is responsive to divine initiative. This fact is modeled by responsive readings of scripture in the call to worship, for example, and in other places as well. Hebrew poetry lends itself to responsive reading, as couplets with parallel meaning are frequently used. The Psalms use this form and many texts may be easily adapted to responsive reading.

There are also refrains that can be sung responsively to a text that may be either read or sung. These are usually referred to as "antiphons." Hymns may be sung responsively too between choir and congregation, between two halves of the congregation, or between men and women of the congregation. "Watchman, Tell Us of the Night" provides an excellent example. (*See also* Antiphon; Call to Worship; Hymn.)

Resurrection.

The resurrection of Jesus Christ is central to Christian worship. Without it there would be no Christian worship. The resurrection validates the whole life and ministry of Jesus Christ and is vivid testimony to the triumph of God over death and evil.

Resurrection is the focus of Easter Day and as such becomes the focus of every Lord's Day. The resurrection of Jesus Christ motivated the selection of the first day of the week as the Lord's Day, and it provides a persistent thematic emphasis. The purpose of preaching is to call the people to new life in Jesus Christ, to die to sin and be alive to what is good.

Resurrection lies at the heart of baptism. The image of baptism is that of dying and being raised to new life in Jesus Christ (see Rom. 6:3–11).

Resurrection is central to our understanding of the Lord's Supper, as distinguished from the Last Supper. The Lord's Supper celebrated on the Lord's Day is derived from the meals the risen Christ shared with his disciples as much as it is from the Last Supper.

Resurrection is the theme of funeral and memorial services as well, where we confront the mystery of death and witness to the resurrection of Jesus Christ and our own. (*See also* Baptism; Easter; Funeral; Lord's Day; Lord's Supper; Preaching/Proclaiming the Word.)

Ritual/Rite.

A *rite* is an action or a ceremony. A *ritual* has to do with the words prescribed for worship. Usually we think of them as synonymous. Religious rites are often based on common human experiences, such as washing in baptism and a meal in the Lord's Supper. In this way rites help us enact our very lives before God.

Although the terms are sometimes used pejoratively in ordinary discussion, even the freest churches develop rites and rituals. They provide a stylized acting out of what is important in our encounter with God. Their repetition can also be valuable, for they become part of people in subconscious ways. The actions and the words take on commonly accepted meanings although these need to be rehearsed so they are not lost. Rites and rituals that are stumbled and mumbled through without conscious content deserve to be abandoned. (*See also* Baptism; Liturgy; Lord's Supper.)

Robe.

See Vestments/Robes/Stoles.

Rubrics.

The term comes from a Latin word for "red coloring" and refers to the liturgical instructions traditionally printed in red in prayer books. Rubrics are sometimes necessary and often helpful. Many churches provide bulletins in which rubrics can be printed. They should be kept to a minimum and as terse as possible so they do not become overly complicated. Directions that people need to see more than once should be printed. Sometimes rubrics can be more effective if given verbally. In either case, simplicity should prevail. There should be enough direction that visitors feel comfortable in participating in the service but not so much as to be overwhelming. (*See also* Announcements; Bulletin.)

Sabbath.

See Lord's Day/Sunday/Sabbath.

Sacrament.

The word *sacrament* is not a biblical term but comes from the Latin *sacramentum*, meaning "oath," referring to the oath of allegiance given by a Roman soldier to Caesar. In worship the sacraments carry this connotation as we make our vows of fidelity to God in baptism and come obediently to the Lord's Table. In this way we rehearse our covenant with God, which is the "new covenant" in Jesus Christ, a fulfillment of the "old covenant" given to Abraham and Sarah and their successors.

The term sacrament also points us to an understanding of God's oath of allegiance to us as well as ours to God, for the covenant is a two-way binding of God with God's people. We trust God to keep promises made in the covenant, promises of a future and peace. The sacraments of baptism and the Lord's Supper are special ways we claim God's promises for ourselves and our children.

In Protestant traditions there are two sacraments, baptism and the Lord's Supper, explicitly commanded by Christ in scripture. The Roman Catholic tradition recognizes five more: marriage, ordination, anointing, penance, and confirmation. In some other traditions, these are recognized as "sacramentals" or "ordinances," rites that are considered means of grace but are not necessary for all the people as are baptism and the Lord's Supper. Some Christian groups, such as the Quakers, do not recognize any sacraments. (See also Baptism; Lord's Supper; Ordinances.)

Saints.

In the New Testament the word *saint* is used to refer to any or all of the people of God (see, for example, Acts 9:41 and Eph. 1:1). The Greek word for *saint* literally means "one being made holy." A saint, therefore, is a forgiven sinner, which means that any of us qualify. Those who know themselves to be forgiven are eager to live a life of holiness. The notion that saints see themselves as "holier-than-thou" is not a biblical thought. Being a saint is not a matter of pride but of devotion.

When we are numbered among the people of God at our baptisms, we become in this sense "saints." It is appropriate for us to celebrate our baptismal days as special times when we entered upon a new life. Congregations may want to structure a way of recording and celebrating the baptismal days of its members to affirm the fellowship of God's people called in grace to be Christ's disciples.

There are other saints, people of exemplary discipleship, heroes and heroines of the church who have gone before us. They are remembered not on their birthdays but on their death days when they entered the "Church Triumphant." Therefore, Martin Luther King, Jr., for example, is remembered in public celebrations on the date of his birthday, January 15, but in the church he is remembered April 4, the day of his assassination. It is appropriate to remember such saints whose witness to the faith encourages us in our time to be loyal followers of Jesus Christ. All Saints' Day (November 1) is a time to remember gratefully in our worship the lives of those gone before us.

Another way to celebrate the saints is to keep a calendar in the church, both of current "saints" by dates of baptisms and of members who have died by the dates of their deaths (at least for the first anniversary of their deaths), along with the heroes and heroines of the faith to be remembered. This calendar might be posted in a prominent place or even noted in the church newsletter or bulletin. (*See also* All Saints' Day; Baptism; Bulletin.)

Salvation History.

Salvation History refers to the mighty acts of God throughout all time. Salvation history is recorded in the Bible. It is also rehearsed liturgically. The Great Prayer of Thanksgiving at the Lord's Supper traditionally has been the primary recitation of salvation history. God is thanked for mighty acts beginning with creation. In this act of grace, God gave life itself. The deliverance of God's people is celebrated in remembering the Exodus. The call of God to all people in the prophets is also thankfully remembered. Supremely, the Christ event (Christ's birth, life, death, resurrection, and ascension) is lifted up as the high point of salvation history. All of this is to remind us that salvation history continues for each of us, that we come to the Lord's Table to partake of his redemption and to look forward to his coming again in the culmination of time.

The Easter Vigil rehearses salvation history by means of a number of readings from scripture. Both baptism (or the renewal of baptism) and the Lord's Supper are celebrated as signs and seals of the covenant in Jesus Christ.

In our worship, we stand in the flow of salvation history. The same God who acted in might long ago is active even now, and that God is at work today moving history toward its ultimate goal, the peace and salvation of all humankind. (*See also* Baptism; Easter Vigil; Great Prayer of Thanksgiving; Lord's Supper; Time.)

Sanctuary.

Originally the word *sanctuary* referred to that part of the worship space reserved for the clergy and perhaps the choir, what is commonly called the chancel today. It is also technically used in some traditions to apply to the area immediately around the altar, especially if it is enclosed by a railing.

Generally today in Protestant churches, sanctuary means the whole worship space. It literally means a "holy space" and suggests that this particular area is set aside for worship of God.

One can worship anywhere, but it is appropriate to claim certain space for worship just as certain times are claimed. It may be helpful to view the sanctuary as a divine beachhead in the world, the beginning of claiming the whole world in the name of Jesus Christ. (*See also* Altar; Chancel; Nave.)

Sanctus.

The Sanctus is also known as the "Holy, Holy, Holy," which is sung or said as part of the Great Prayer of Thanksgiving in the Lord's Supper. It is the song of the angels to which we join our voices in praising God for the gift of Jesus Christ. The text comes from Isaiah 6:3, the words sung at the divine throne in Isaiah's vision of God. This song is echoed in John's vision recorded in Revelation 4:8.

The Sanctus as used in the Christian church combines these ancient songs with the praise given Jesus at his entrance into Jerusalem (see Matt. 21:9 and Luke 19:38), which comes from Psalm 118:25–26. Musical settings for the Sanctus are found in most hymnals. (*See also* Great Prayer of Thanksgiving; Lord's Supper.)

Scripture.

See Bible/Scripture/Word of God; Lectionary; Lesson.

Season.

The Christian year has a number of seasons around the major festivals of Christmas and Easter. Advent is the season preceding Christmas, and Lent is the season preceding Easter. Each holy day is followed by a season of its own. The rest of the year is designated "ordinary time."

Seasons of the Christian year mark the journey of faith through the life of Christ. The changing of colors for seasons and special days enables worshipers to have a sense of movement. Worship is dynamic, not static. In worship we are on our way toward God's goal, and we travel through time.

The seasons of the Christian year have parallels in the times of one's life. The longings and yearnings of Advent, the gift of life at Christmas, the struggles and sorrows of Lent, and the new life of Easter all touch human experience deeply. The seasons do not simply mark a progression through a church calendar but help us find our own ways through our journeys of faith. (*See also* Advent; Christian Year; Christmas; Colors; Easter; Lent; Ordinary Time; Time.)

Sending.

See Benediction.

Sentences of Scripture.

See Call to Worship.

Sermon.

See Preaching/Proclaiming the Word.

Service for the Lord's Day.

Service for the Lord's Day is a commonly accepted term for Sunday worship including Word and sacrament. The classic order of worship in Christian churches has these two parts:

1. The service of the *word* centers on the proclamation of God's Word in scripture and sermon, with acts of praise and confession in preparation for receiving God's Word.
2. The service of the *sacrament* centers on the enactment of God's Word in the Lord's Supper, with acts of commitment in response to God's Word.

In both cases, the Word of God spoken in Jesus Christ (John 1:14) is proclaimed and enacted.

In Protestant worship generally the emphasis has fallen primarily on the Word proclaimed in scripture and sermon. In comparison, the sacrament of the Lord's Supper has tended to be neglected.

Just before the Protestant Reformation, the sacrament of the Lord's Supper was celebrated as frequently as each day. However, the people saw it as a miracle to be viewed from a respectful distance, not as something in which they could participate. The result was that they received Communion infrequently, to the point that it became a requirement for every believer to receive the sacrament at least once a year. Easter was the occasion for the mandatory annual Communion.

Most of the Reformers were convinced that the Lord's Supper should be celebrated each Lord's Day. It was unrealistic, however, to think that the people could move immediately from once a year to once a week, so concessions were made to accommodate a less frequent observance, usually quarterly. Most Protestants settled for this pattern of infrequency, which has been perpetuated into this century. Even though John Calvin never got weekly Communion, he was convinced that the people should share the Lord's Supper each Lord's Day to maintain the classical balance of Word and sacrament.

The order of service usually reflects this twofold pattern, whether or not the sacrament is observed. The first part may be thought of as getting ready for hearing God's Word in scripture. The second part may be thought of as responding to God's Word in scripture by obedient acts, preeminently obeying Christ's commands to eat and drink in the Lord's Supper (1 Cor. 11:23–25). The order of worship, then, looks like this:

Service of the Word

Gathering for Worship
Call to Worship
   Hymn
   Prayer of the Day
   [Anthem of praise]
Preparing in Confession
   Prayer of Confession, unison and silent
   Declaration of God's Forgiveness
      Praise
Proclamation of Scripture
   Prayer for Illumination
   Reading of Old Testament
      Response from Psalter
   New Testament and Gospel Lessons
   Sermon

Service of the Sacrament

Affirmation of Faith
   Creed
   Hymn
   [Baptism]
Concerns [Announcements]
Prayers of the People/Intercessions

Offering [Anthem]
Lord's Supper
    Great Prayer of Thanksgiving
       concluding with the Lord's Prayer
    Breaking of the Bread
    Communion of the People
    Prayer after Communion
Hymn
    Charge and Benediction

The particular order of the service of worship on a Sunday is ordinarily determined by appropriate lay leaders in consultation with the pastor. Sometimes the pastor has more authority in this area although a close working relationship with the lay leadership of the church is always necessary.

In determining the order of service the following should be considered: (a) fidelity to the biblical faith; (b) awareness of the Christian tradition of worship through the centuries, especially the particular tradition that forms the heritage of the particular church; (c) the experience and involvement of the worshiping congregation; and (d) the progression and relationship of the various elements.

The order of service has some flexibility. There are options that may be added or subtracted without damage to the integrity of the order. While pastoral considerations may require shifting some elements from time to time, the reasons for such adjustments will need to be thought through clearly and carefully. The balance of Word and sacrament in the general pattern of Christian worship has centuries of tradition behind it and should not be ignored. (*See also* Anthem; Baptism; Bible/Scripture/Word of God; Call to Worship; Hymn; Lord's Supper; Prayer; Preaching/Proclaiming the Word; Worship.)

Service for Wholeness.

It is increasingly common for churches to hold "healing services" or "services for wholeness." This reflects the church's perennial concern for the total well-being of people.

It is important to realize that such services are not the manipulation of God in some magical way. Healing is not claimed on the basis of the piety, righteousness, or zeal of the participants but awaited as a gift from God in the power of the Holy Spirit. Physical healing, then, is to be understood in the context of the healing of the brokenness of the whole person. In Jesus Christ the broken are made whole and brought once again into right relationship with God. The promise of spiritual wholeness is claimed in a service of wholeness. It is not that sickness and death are to be avoided but that they are ultimately overcome by Christ's redemption. When physical healing happens, it is the result of God's grace and normally comes through those who serve God in healing ministries.

In the life of any congregation, there will be opportunity to join in prayers for those who are in specific need of wholeness, not only the sick, but the sorrowing as well, and those who suffer from broken relationships. Prayer is the main part of a service of wholeness as the community stands together before God. Thanksgiving for God's redemption in Jesus Christ, intercessions for those in need, and the silence of waiting are characteristic of the prayers. It is appropriate that scripture be read and proclaimed in sermon so that the healing Word who is Christ may be recognized. The Lord's Supper may be celebrated as well, and baptismal vows renewed. The laying on of hands and anointing with oil are also appropriate acts for such a service. (*See also* Anointing; Intercession; Laying on of Hands; Lord's Supper; Renewal of Baptism; Silence.)

Signs.

See Symbols.

Silence.

We have grown so accustomed to sound in our lives that silence is often considered an embarrassment. This need not be so, especially in worship. Silence, as Quakers well know, is not a time for inactivity. Silence provides opportunity for meditation and contemplation, for prayer that is listening as well as speaking, for being open to the movement of the Spirit of God. When we have no time for silence, we run the risk of preempting God's Spirit.

There are several points at which silence can play an important part in our worship. The first is at the prayer of confession. There should always be a time for silent prayers of personal confession so worshipers have time to internalize their prayers and appropriate for themselves the forgiveness of God.

A second place for silence is at the prayers of intercession and petition. Silence offers the chance for worshipers to particularize the prayers for others, visualizing those people for whom they have concern and listening for the guidance of Holy Spirit in how to reach out in love.

Another time when silence can be helpful is immediately following the reading of scripture, when the Word revealed can have a chance to be absorbed and contemplated personally. This is good preparation for the worshiper to participate in the sermon.

Similarly, when the Lord's Supper is served, silence may occasionally be helpful in enabling the worshipers' meditation as they appropriate the gift of Jesus Christ in the breaking of bread and the sharing of wine.

Silence may be helpful at other points in the service as well. Care should be given to allow it to happen, to interpret it as necessary, and to resist the temptation to provide verbal or musical interludes to fill what we fear might be awkward blanks. (*See also* Confession of Sin; Intercession, Meditation; Lord's Supper.)

Solemn Intercessions.

See Intercession; Good Friday.

Solemn Reproaches from the Cross.

The Solemn Reproaches from the Cross (often simply called "the Reproaches") come from a tenth-century French text associated with Good Friday. They represent Christ as reproaching the people for their ingratitude for God's mighty acts of deliverance, as evidenced by their rejection of him as the Messiah.

The Reproaches are often used in place of a prayer of confession, and after each one a refrain may be sung or said by the congregation, either a simple "Lord, have mercy" or the Kyrie, Trisagion, or other response.

Some have expressed concern that the Reproaches display an antisemitism unworthy of Christian worship. It should be clear that the Reproaches are not aimed at the Jews but at the followers of Jesus. The modern counterparts of those who crucified Jesus are not Jewish people at all but Christian church members. At the foot of the cross on Good Friday we all confess our complicity in the crucifixion, even as we allow truth, righteousness, and justice to be crucified in our own time. Many denominations are producing modern versions of the Reproaches that make this point very clear.

The Reproaches should be pronounced solemnly and heard carefully in the heart. (*See also* Confession of Sin; Good Friday; Kyrie; Trisagion.)

Song.

Singing has always been integral to Christian worship, providing, as it does, a form of expression to God for the deepest longings and celebrations of the human heart. Liturgical song takes many forms. In addition to hymns, the congregation may sing responses, Psalms, doxologies, and even parts of the liturgy itself (the Lord's Prayer and the creed, for example). Choirs may sing anthems, songs of praise, and songs of proclamation on behalf of all worshipers. Songs representing many cultures, races, and nationalities reflect the diversity of God's people in praise. (*See also* Anthem; Chant; Doxology; Hymn; Music; Psalms; Spirituals.)

Speaking in Tongues.

See Ecstatic Utterances/Speaking in Tongues.

Spirituals.

The term *spiritual* is usually applied to a song from the African-American Christian experience.

Because spirituals come from the experience unique to African Americans, they contribute a sensitivity to human suffering different from other religious songs. A longing for justice and freedom pervades spirituals, communicating a historical message as well as a theological one.

Spirituals reflect particular insights into the Christian faith inspired by the power of the Holy Spirit. The redemption of Jesus Christ is celebrated in these songs with authenticity. Their content is often profound, celebrating at once the joy of the gospel and the depth of human suffering.

Spirituals are related to other folk music, and so have a simplicity that makes them very singable. Their rhythms are exciting, and they readily involve the worshiper in singing and feeling the faith. (*See also* Hymn; Music; Song.)

Sponsors.

In some traditions, sponsors rather than godparents are designated for persons being baptized. In the Reformed tradition, members of the congregation are considered sponsors of baptized infants and adults, assuming or assisting in the responsibility of nurture and development of the person's Christian faith on behalf of the whole church of Jesus Christ. More recently, Presbyterian churches have designated sponsors, specific individuals who are themselves baptized Christians and active in that particular church. This allows for the personification of congregational concern for the person baptized. Sponsors are named by action of the governing board in consultation with those desiring baptism for themselves or their children. (*See also* Baptism.)

Stole.

See Vestments/Robes/Stoles.

Sunday.

See Lord's Day/Sunday/Sabbath.

Sursum Corda.

Sursum corda comes from the Latin for "Lift up your hearts" and refers to a liturgical dialogue at the beginning of the Great Prayer of Thanksgiving at the Lord's Supper. It dates back to at least the second century and is one of the oldest parts of Christian liturgy still in use.

The sentence is often part of a dialogue in which two lines, known as the Dominus vobiscum, Latin for "The Lord be with you," are spoken by the one presiding and followed by another two lines, the Gratias agamus, Latin for "Let us give thanks," which introduce the Great Prayer of Thanksgiving. The full dialogue between the one presiding at the Lord's Table and the congregation is often referred to collectively as the Sursum Corda.

> The Lord be with you.
> And also with you.
> Lift up your hearts.
> We lift them up to the Lord.
> Let us give thanks to the Lord our God.
> It is right to give God thanks and praise.

(*See also* Great Prayer of Thanksgiving; Lord's Supper.)

Symbols.

There are always symbols in the church. Distinction has been made between signs and symbols, the former being mere conventional representations that stand for something, while symbols carry the essence of that which they represent. Such distinctions are debatable and are not made in biblical writings, where signs and symbols function in the same way. In either case, symbols point beyond themselves to a greater reality. Symbols provide helpful reminders of the complexity of our faith and highlight significant themes and even doctrines. Gestures and postures are often symbolic, carrying specific meanings and involving the worshiper physically in expressing faith.

Numbers are often important and are used to point to numerical usage in scripture and in the doctrines of the church. The following are some common meanings attached to numbers used in Christian symbolism:

1 stands for the One God.

2 is the number most often associated with Christ, referring to his divine and human natures (the two candles on either side of the pulpit, for example, stand for Christ).

3 indicates the Trinity or may refer to Holy Spirit, the third person of the Trinity. It may also refer to the three crosses on Calvary or the three days Christ spent in the tomb.

4 stands for the earth, the four corners of the earth, or the four directions. It is the number of completeness. Four also refers to the four Gospels.

5 signifies the wounds of Christ on the cross, in each hand, both feet, and the side. It also represents the number of points on the Epiphany star to distinguish that from the star of David, which has six points.

6 is the number for creation, God having accomplished that work in six days. The star of David has six points.

7 is the holiest of all numbers, referring to the Sabbath and to the seven gifts of the Spirit.

8 is the number for resurrection or new life in Christ, the day of resurrection being the "eighth day of creation." Baptismal fonts are often eight-sided to emphasize the resurrection.

9 is three-times-three and stands for the Trinity.

10 is a reminder of the Ten Commandments or the Law of God.

11 refers to the faithful disciples (minus Judas).

12 refers to the disciples as selected by Jesus (after Judas' betrayal and death, the disciples replaced him to keep the

number at twelve). Twelve also refers to the twelve tribes of
Israel, and it is suggested that Jesus selected twelve disciples
to indicate that they represented the whole of the people of
Israel (see Matt. 19:28).

13 is sometimes considered to be unlucky because there
were thirteen people at table at the Last Supper.

40 is a number applied to time: Jesus spent forty days in
the wilderness, the people of Israel wandered forty years in
the wilderness, Noah's flood resulted from forty days and
forty nights of rain, for example. It is a round number and
refers to a long period of time. Forty years was thought to
have been the approximate length of a generation.

70 is formed by the multiplication of two sacred numbers
(seven and ten) and was noted as the number of years of the
Babylonian captivity. Jesus sent out seventy people as his disciples (Luke 10:1). Seventy times seven was a round number
used by Jesus to indicate a number beyond calculation (Matt.
18:22).

1000 is a round number applied to years, indicating God's
view of time as being eternal. It is used to denote the millen-
nium, the end of time.

Graphic symbols are important visual aids. They communicate instantaneously a biblical story or event and often express a Christian truth. The following are some Christian
symbols more commonly used in worship or the decoration
of worship space.

Alpha and Omega, the first and last letters of the Greek
alphabet (similar to a capital *A* and an inverted *U*), are reminders of Christ's statement about himself being the first
and last, the beginning and the end (Rev. 1:8).

Ark of Noah signifies Christian baptism as deliverance by
water and also the church.

Branch stands for Jesus Christ, as prophesied in
Zechariah 3:8, and also the church as indicated in Jesus' com-
ment, "I am the vine, you are the branches" (John 15:5).

Burning Bush represents the appearance of God to Moses (Exod. 3:1–6), and is sometimes used as a symbol for the nativity of Jesus Christ.

Butterfly points to the resurrection because a caterpillar is "dead" in the cocoon and then comes forth as a completely new creature. In particular, the caterpillar is sometimes used to represent the human condition, the cocoon the grave, and the butterfly the resurrected body.

Candle stands for Jesus Christ who said, "I am the light of the world" (John 8:12). When two candles are used, they represent Christ's divine and human natures.

Chi Rho are the first two letters of Christ in Greek (similar to the capital letters X and P). Often combined in a monogram, the two letters are an abbreviation used out of reverence for Christ.

Crown of Thorns signifies the suffering and crucifixion of Christ.

Crown of Royalty signifies the sovereignty of Jesus Christ.

Dove, Descending, represents the Holy Spirit, who descended at the time of Christ's baptism (Matt. 3:13–17; Mark 1:9–11; Luke 3:21–22; John 1:31–34).

Fish is a statement of faith, the Greek word for fish (*ichthus*) being an acronym representing the first letters of the Greek words that mean, "Jesus Christ, God's Son, Savior." The symbol in its simplest form of two curved lines joined at one end and crossing, was used by early Christians under persecution as a sign of mutual identification; one person would draw the first line, and the other would complete the drawing.

Flames represent the Holy Spirit, according to the Pentecost narrative in Acts 2:1–4.

Fleur-de-Lis is a stylized form of the lily, sometimes used to point to the human nature of Christ at his birth, or to the Virgin Mary, and more often as a symbol for the Trinity.

IHS is an abbreviation for the name "Jesus" in Greek. It was used in writing as a sign of reverence for the Lord rather than spelling the name out in full. This is similar to the Jewish practice of refraining from spelling out (or even pronouncing) Yahweh, the name of God.

INRI stands for *Iesus Nazarenus Rex Iudaeorum*, which is Latin for "Jesus of Nazareth, King of the Jews," the inscription Pontius Pilate placed on Jesus' cross.

Jesse Tree, derived from Isaiah 11:1, points to the birth of Christ as a descerdant of Jesse. It is like a "family tree" of Jesus, showing his lineage.

Lamb, when pictured with a nimbus and cross, refers to the Lamb of God (see John 1:29).

Lilies are associated with Easter because they bloom at that time of year and because their bulbs appear to be dead before they grow and bloom.

Locust and Honey are symbols of John the Baptist, recalling his diet.

Menorah is a seven-branched candlestick of Jewish origin used in Christian symbolism to represent the seven gifts of the Holy Spirit.

Nails, usually three, represent the crucifixion.

Nimbus, like a halo, signifies sanctity and is applied to persons of exceptional piety. A three-rayed nimbus is used only for persons of the Trinity.

Orb symbolizes the world. With a cross on top it indicates the triumph of Christ over the sinfulness of the world.

Peacock is a symbol of renewal and resurrection. According to legend the peacock sheds its plumes only to grow more beautiful ones.

Pelican is a striking representation of Christ's sacrificial love. According to legend, in times of famine, the pelican tears open her skin to feed her young with her own blood.

Phoenix is a legendary bird that, every four or five centuries builds a nest that catches fire from the sun and burns the phoenix. The bird then rises anew from the ashes, obviously a symbol of the resurrection.

Pomegranate signifies the resurrection because it has seeds that burst forth in proliferating new life as Christ burst forth from the tomb. Also, because of its many seeds in one fruit, the pomegranate is often used to symbolize the church as a unity of many in one Lord.

Rooster or a crowing cock signifies Peter's denial of Jesus (Matt. 26:69–75).

Rose has many meanings: the Messiah (see Isa. 35:1, KJV); the nativity of Jesus Christ; a white rose, the Virgin Mary; a red rose, martyrdom or the death of Christ; love.

Scepter, the royal staff, signifies the sovereignty of Jesus Christ, based on Numbers 24:17.

Serpent indicates the temptation and fall of Adam and Eve. A very different meaning is found in the story of Moses raising up a serpent in the wilderness (Num. 21:4–9), which was noted by Jesus as being a prototype of his crucifixion (John 3:14–15).

Shell, with drops of water, is a symbol of baptism.

Ship, usually with a cross on the mast, represents the church, sailing on its mission, powered by the wind of the Spirit. This symbol is also seen in the use of the word *nave* (from the Latin word for ship) for worship space.

Stars. The Star of David, a six-pointed star fashioned from two overlapping triangles, in Christian symbolism points to Jesus as a descendant of the House of David. Its six points also refer to the six days of creation, and it is sometimes called "the Star of Creation." The *Star of Epiphany,* usually five-pointed, is the star followed by the Magi from the east to Bethlehem (Matt. 2:2).

Sun represents Christ and usually contains a monogram of Christ (see Mal. 4:2).

Thirty Coins are the pieces of silver given to Judas and represent his betrayal of Christ (Matt. 26:14–15).

Trumpet may signify the resurrection, judgment day, or simply the call to worship.

YHWH is the four-letter name of God, transliterated from Hebrew. In Christian usage this is sometimes spelled out as YaHWeH or JeHoVaH. Most Bible translations substitute LORD, following the Jewish practice of abbreviating God's name in print and using a substitute word, *Adonai* or "Lord," when speaking, out of reverence for the One Holy God.

(*See also* Nave; Font.)

Table.

The table is the focal center of Christian worship, representing the Lord's Table around which the family of faith gathers for the Lord's Supper.

The table is not the same as an "altar." The Reformers did not accept the theology represented by an altar that suggested the repetition of the sacrifice of Jesus Christ. Therefore, they insisted that the table be obviously a table on which a meal might be served.

It should be readily apparent that the function of the table in the place of worship is to serve the communion meal. Each Sunday when the sacrament is not observed, it is still appropriate to set the table with communion ware (without the elements). (*See also* Altar; Lord's Supper.)

Tenebrae.

The word *tenebrae* is Latin for "shadows" and is used with reference to the gathering shadows of the Maundy Thursday–Good Friday events. A Tenebrae service is sometimes used on Maundy Thursday. Candles are extinguished throughout the service as readings from scripture tell the story leading up to the crucifixion. The room becomes darker and darker until at last only the Christ candle is left burning. The people depart in darkness to return for Good Friday worship that rehearses the crucifixion.

The Tenebrae service is balanced by the Easter Vigil, which has just the opposite effect, as successive candles are lighted with the readings from scripture of events from salvation history, culminating in the resurrection of Jesus Christ. (*See also* Candles; Easter Vigil; Good Friday; Maundy Thursday; Paschal Candle; Salvation History.)

Thanksgiving.

Thanksgiving is at the heart of Christian worship. All we do in worship is essentially give thanks to God for our creation and recreation in Jesus Christ. The Great Prayer of Thanksgiving used in the Lord's Supper is a rehearsal of God's mighty acts of grace, especially in the death and resurrection of Jesus Christ. The thanksgiving over the water in baptism similarly recalls God's acts of deliverance of God's people from death to life.

Thanksgiving is often thought of as simply one form of prayer. Yet it underlies every form. Praise is always a thankful response for God's grace. Confession gratefully presumes God's acceptance, forgiveness, and reconciliation. Intercession asks for others what one has thankfully received for oneself. Petitionary prayer is but a grateful response to God's mercies in the past.

Thanksgiving as national holidays in the United States and Canada is an opportunity for us to be grateful not only for the blessings of our country but also to recognize the blessings from God for all people.

Thanksgiving always moves us to action. For what we have come to appreciate from God is worth working to preserve and to gain for ourselves and for others. Thanksgiving is never to suggest being smug but to motivate us to mission in the name of Jesus Christ. Thanksgiving provokes us to generosity. As we have received of God's generosity, so we will give to others. (*See also* Baptism; Great Prayer of Thanksgiving; Mission; Prayer; Prayer of Thanksgiving.)

Time.

There are two kinds of time. *Chronos*, chronological time, is sequential, marked off by clocks and calendars. In this time, one thing happens after another. It is the time of history. *Chronos* is one of the Greek words for time.

There is another word in Greek for time, *kairos*. This is not the same as chronological time but is related to it. *Kairos* is the significant moment when something happens that gives meaning to chronological time.

Baseball provides us with imagery to understand the two kinds of time. The box score, inning by inning, is a display of *chronos*, showing the sequence of events, the "history" of the ball game. The *kairos* of the game, however, may have been the double play in the second inning that kept a run from scoring and was ultimately recognized as the "play of the game."

Chronos is the history of humankind from creation to culmination, from Genesis to Revelation, the story of God's purposeful love. It is the gospel, the "Good Story," because of *kairos* events recognized by people of faith. These events give ultimate meaning to the chronology.

If we look at the chronology of human history, we recognize certain *kairos* events, times when God broke into history to do something that we know affected the outcome, that moved history toward God's goal. The creation itself is understood to be an act of love and mercy by Almighty God. The deliverance of Noah from the flood waters is also significant, as is the call of Abraham. The Passover and Exodus stand out as a supreme *kairos* while many others can be added to the list. For Christians, however, the only *kairos* that matters is the Christ event (the birth, life, death, resurrection, and ascension of Jesus Christ). In this single life, God acted in such a way as to guarantee the outcome of human history to be good and in accord with God's promises. This was the "play" that will be ultimately recognized as having "won the game," even though it is not over yet.

In worship we deal with both kinds of time. The order of service provides a sense of *chronos*. Yet we come to worship expecting God to break through and do whatever it is we need to redeem the time and make it significant. We believe that Holy Spirit works in worship in *kairos*. Holy Spirit makes a phrase from the sermon take hold in our hearts, or a song of the choir stir our souls, or the touch of a friend to be the touch of God's love. We never know when *kairos* will take place, but we expect it and look for it.

Worship, then, is that experience when *kairos* and *chronos* intersect, when God intrudes into the normal sequence of things and makes something special happen. When God intrudes, we lose a sense of chronological time. The length of the service becomes not only unimportant but unnoticed. For the *kairos* of God's breaking in is seen to be eternal time, time without end, time that is measured not in duration but in quality. *Kairos* is the ultimately significant moment in which we experience the eternal and are touched by God.

The *kairos* will, therefore, affect everything else. Chronological time, including what we will do when we leave church, and what happens Monday and Tuesday and the rest of the week, has new meaning for it is recognized as God's time too, and it is tinged with the eternal.

Experience of the *kairos* makes us aware of other *chronos* times in which we live and how they are redeemed by God. People of faith view history not simply as *chronos* but as a series of *kairos* events.

The life of each person is chronological, but each of us recognizes those significant moments, those *kairos* events that have given meaning to our lives and maybe even directed the course of them. Often we can point to one experience among the many that was of ultimate significance, a moment when God broke through for us, an incident that left us with the certainty of the meaning of our lives, a time when we were touched by the eternal, something that happened which we recognized then or later to have been God redeeming us for God's own purpose. We come to worship bringing these chronologies and these *kairos* experiences with us.

The year flows chronologically, and the Christian year connects that *chronos* to the *kairos* of the Christ-event. Advent counts down four Sundays to Christmas, and then there are twelve days to celebrate the birth of Christ. Lent leads us through a preparation period for Holy Week and Easter, when there are fifty days to experience the joy of it. Even "ordinary time" is not mundane but gives a basic progression of time and serves to lead us from one major festival cycle to the other. When we come to worship, we are conscious of being at a certain point in that sequence of events, that *chronos*, and aware of what God has done. In worship we go through the sequence of events, alert to God's *kairos* that might happen at any moment.

The week has a flow from Sunday to Saturday, from the first to the last day. Each day is connected in Christian thought with the events of Holy Week, and thus tied to the *kairos* of the crucifixion and resurrection of Jesus Christ. We come to worship on the resurrection day, celebrating that ultimate breakthrough of God into human history in Christ's victory over death. Each day moves from evening to night to morning to day, and our Lord's Day worship is in the context of our daily worship. Some Christians begin Sunday on Saturday evening with their time of worship, while others wait until early morning and others until late morning or even afternoon or evening. The sequence of the day is connected in Christian thought with the divine *kairos*, as evening reflects on the day gone by and anticipates the day to come; night remembers our death and the entrusting of our lives to God; morning celebrates the resurrection, and the day witnesses to the presence of the risen Christ. When we gather with the community to worship God, we are conscious of the *chronos* of the day.

Time itself is a gift of God, and the time we have is a sign of God's grace and patience with us. Time is what we use for God. What is important is not how much time we use, but how we use all of it. It is the quality of time that counts, not its quantity. That is determined by our ability to recognize God's eternity breaking into our minutes and hours, days and years.

Chronos and *kairos* represent for us the paradox of the timely and the eternal. As we live from day to day through the course of our years, we recognize the eternal presence of God, who gives meaning and direction to our lives. It is only as we see the eternal quality of time that we live life to its fullest. (*See also* Christian Year; Holy Week; Ordinary Time; Salvation History; Season; Service for the Lord's Day; Worship.)

Triduum.

Triduum is from the Latin, meaning "three days" and refers to Maundy Thursday, Good Friday, and Holy Saturday (including Easter Vigil). It is during these three days that the whole of the Christian faith comes into sharpest focus around the crucifixion of Jesus Christ. The observances of the three days fit together, telling in dramatic fashion the story of Christ.

Maundy Thursday, Good Friday, and Easter Vigil each need the others to tell the full story. Services for the three may be included in a single bulletin to emphasize this point.

The *Triduum* is also known as the "Great Three Days," or the "Three Holy Days," and is respected as the holiest time of the Christian year. (*See also* Easter Vigil; Good Friday; Holy Saturday; Maundy Thursday.)

Trinity.

See Father, Son, and Holy Spirit.

Trinity Sunday.

The Sunday following Pentecost is Trinity Sunday. This day celebrates a doctrine rather than an event or person and so is different in character from other special days in the year. On this day we affirm the triune God in whose name we are baptized, the same God revealed in Scripture to be One God in Three Persons, Father, Son, and Holy Spirit. (*See also* Father, Son, and Holy Spirit; God; Jesus Christ; Holy Spirit; Language of Worship.)

Trisagion.

Trisagion is from the Latin for "thrice holy" and refers to a brief fifth-century hymn from Constantinople:

> Holy God,
> Holy and Mighty,
> Holy and immortal One,
> Have mercy upon us.

It is used in Western churches primarily as a response to the reproaches on Good Friday. The Trisagion may also be used as an alternative to the Kyrie in response to the prayer of confession. (*See also* Confession of Sin; Good Friday; Kyrie; Solemn Reproaches from the Cross.)

Vestments/Robes/Stoles.

At the time of the Protestant Reformation, Calvinists reacted strongly to the proliferation of statuary in churches, ornate architecture, and clerical vestments, which they saw as a distraction from the main emphasis in worship, namely the proclamation of God's Word and the administration of the sacraments. The excessive and elaborate ceremonial color that went with it was considered to be of human origin, calling attention to the human participants at the expense of the true worship of God.

English Puritans intensified this reaction and brought it to this country with a vengeance. Churches were simple in architecture, often little more than a meeting house. Statuary was absent, of course, but so was all symbolism or color. Vestments were reduced to somber black robes. The visual focus was to be on the open Bible and the Lord's Table.

In recent years, many Protestants have begun carefully to reclaim some of the larger heritage of the church, discovering that color and symbols can be aids to worship and need not be distracting.

A few generations ago, common attire for many a Protestant minister in this country was striped trousers and a morning coat or other dignified gentlemanly attire (there were no women clergy in the major denominations then). Traditionally, Reformed clergy also wore the pulpit robe, sometimes referred to as a "Geneva gown," after the town in Switzerland where Calvin preached. This was an academic gown worn to signify the education of the clergy but also to efface the personality of the pastor so the focus was on the Word rather than the preacher.

White robes are also considered appropriate in some traditions to signify the one who administers the sacraments, as the black designates the preacher of the Word. Today Protestant pastors often wear white robes, usually in the form of an alb, as most appropriate to the celebration of the resurrection each Lord's Day. The alb is a full-length garment that finds its origin in ancient times and is often considered basic to religious vestments.

A chasuble is derived from a cloaklike garment worn in ancient times. The word *chasuble* comes from a word meaning "little house" and refers to its tentlike shape. Chasubles are often colorfully decorated according to the season of the Christian year.

Stoles are often worn around the shoulders of the pastor as the symbol of the yoke of Christ. Stoles provide a fine opportunity for displaying symbols and color appropriate to the season or special day. (*See also* Christian Year; Colors; Lesson; Symbols.)

Wedding.

See Marriage.

Wine.

See Bread/Wine.

Word of God.

See Bible/Scripture/Word of God.

Words of Institution.

See Institution, Words of.

Worship.

Worship is literally "ascribing worth" to God. What we do in worship represents an awareness of the relationship between ourselves and God. We are creatures and God is the Creator of us and our world. We exist at the will of God, and we are confident that God's will is for our good. So we worship God, affirming our faith in God as the ultimate value in life. Worship is our encounter with God in response to God's promised presence in Jesus Christ.

Worship is both corporate and private. Not only does each of us reach out to God in personal ways, but all of us together worship God as a people.

Worship is an acknowledgment of human need. By worshiping God, we admit that we are not self-sufficient but utterly dependent on the grace of God for our sustenance and our salvation. By worshiping God together in the community of faith, we proclaim that we are interdependent with one another in the unity of the Holy Spirit.

Worship is also public because the One whom we worship has loved us and all people, and that is Good News we want to share. Christians need to be aware that their going to church on a Sunday morning is a witness to the world around them, starting with their neighbors. It points to life's values revealed by God in Jesus Christ, and it identifies God's people as promoters of those values. (*See also* Congregation; God; Good News; Time.)

Worship Committee.

Every congregation does well to have a worship committee, whether a formal committee established by and reporting to the governing board, or an informal group of people with particular interest in worship meeting with the pastor. The main purpose of the worship committee is to provide a vehicle for reviewing the worship life of the congregation and proposing changes.

The worship committee should include members of the governing board, members of the congregation at-large, church school teachers, musicians, artists, and the pastor. The committee looks at worship in the congregation, particularly the Lord's Day service. In evaluating the congregation's worship, attention should be given to active participation of the congregation in worship and the focus of worship on God. The committee may also plan courses, workshops, or other events to provide education in worship for adults as well as for children and young people.

The worship committee may recommend to the governing board of the congregation such policies as may be helpful to the community's worship life. Suggestions about the desirability of funerals in the church, the use of the pall, and the closing of the casket are examples of policies on funerals that might be recommended. More general matters, such as restrictions on photography during worship services, may also be considered.

One of the more important functions of a worship committee is to facilitate the participation of lay people in the planning of worship experiences. Members of the committee should themselves be involved in planning on a broad scale and should gather others to plan specific services and worship events. Children and young people should be included in this process from time to time. Working with the pastor, the lay planners should shape the service around the biblical or seasonal theme, select hymns, determine the substance of prayers, and participate in the leadership of the service. The preacher may welcome insights shared by worship planners to stimulate sermonic preparation. (*See also* Congregation; Laity/Lay Reader/Lay Leader; Service for the Lord's Day; Worship.)

X.

This symbol is the Greek letter "chi," the first letter of "Christ" when written in Greek. "X," therefore, stands for Christ. Sometimes is used reverently in liturgical designs on stoles or banners. It more often appears less reverently in secular seasonal displays referring to Christmas as "X-mas." (*See also* Cross; Jesus Christ; Symbols.)

FOR FURTHER READING

The list that follows is admittedly subjective. These resources have been and continue to be helpful in my understanding of worship. Readers may find them stimulating and useful for further study.

Basic Resources

Supplemental Liturgical Resource Series (Louisville: Westminster/John Knox Press): *The Service for the Lord's Day* (SLR 1); *Holy Baptism and Services for the Renewal of Baptism* (SLR 2); *Christian Marriage* (SLR 3); *The Funeral: A Service of Witness to the Resurrection* (SLR 4); *Daily Prayer* (SLR 5); *Services for Occasions of Pastoral Care* (SLR 6); *Liturgical Year* (SLR 7). The essays accompanying the liturgies provide excellent background and interpretive material regarding worship in the Reformed tradition. The full set is a valuable resource for the church library and pastor's study. Worship committees will find them useful in many regards. *Study Guides* are available for the first four volumes.

Hickman, Hoyt L., et al., eds. *Handbook of the Christian Year*. Nashville: Abingdon Press, 1986. Full of contemporary liturgies for the Christian year, this handbook also provides a wealth of information about special days and seasons.

Books for Reading and Study

Baillie, D. M., *Theology of the Sacraments*. New York:

Charles Scribner's Sons, 1957. Sacramental theology is interpreted from the Reformed perspective in this classic.

Buechner, Frederick. *Telling the Truth: The Gospel as Tragedy, Comedy, and Fairy Tale.* New York: Harper and Row, 1977. The essence of preaching is captured in this eloquent and readable volume. Buechner offers insights to lay people about the awe and anxiety of preaching, and plenty of encouragement and challenge to the preacher.

Daniels, Harold. *What to Do with Sunday Morning.* Louisville: Westminster/John Knox Press, 1979. This slim volume, overflowing with practical suggestions and insights, will be useful to worship committees and pastors, as well as to the general reader.

Davies, J. G., ed. *The New Westminster Dictionary of Liturgy and Worship.* Philadelphia: Westminster Press, 1986. The most comprehensive and best reference work on worship available, this dictionary includes entries and brief essays on virtually every aspect of worship in every tradition.

Erickson, Craig Douglas. *Participating in Worship: History, Theory, and Practice.* Louisville: Westminster/John Knox Press, 1989. Filled with practical information, this book makes a welcome addition to resources available to worship committees and pastors. It has a built-in study guide, which enhances its usefulness for educational programs and for the general reader.

Schmemann, Alexander. *For the Life of the World: The Sacraments and Orthodoxy.* New York: St Vladimir's Seminary Press, 1973. This clear and inspiring book on the sacraments from the Orthodox perspective has much to offer Christians of all traditions.

Webber, Robert E. *Worship Old and New.* Grand Rapids: Zondervan Publishing House, 1982. This book was written as a college or seminary text, but it is also helpful to pastors, worship committees, and interested lay people. It is clearly written and comprehensive.

White, James F. *Sacraments as God's Self Giving.* Nashville: Abingdon Press, 1983. A fresh approach to the sacraments dealing with current practical issues as well as theology, this book is of interest to lay people and pastors.

Willimon, William H. *Word, Water, Wine and Bread.* Valley Forge, Pa: Judson Press, 1980. This book presents a brief historical survey of Christian worship and sees liturgical renewal in terms of the renewal of the church.

For Advanced Study

Dix, Gregory. *The Shape of the Liturgy.* London: Dacre Press, Adam & Charles Black, 1945. This classic provides a detailed chronicle of the development of Christian worship.

Jones, Cheslyn, et al., eds. *The Study of Liturgy.* New York: Oxford University Press, 1978. This outstanding collection of scholarly essays deals with the history and theology of worship from many perspectives.

Schmemann, Alexander. *Introduction to Liturgical Theology.* New York: St. Vladimir's Seminary Press, 1966. A primer on liturgical theology from the hand of one of the best in the field, this brief book is well worth reading.

Wainwright, Geoffrey. *Doxology: The Praise of God in Worship, Doctrine, and Life.* New York: Oxford University Press, 1980. This is a systematic theology from the perspective of liturgy, an important contribution to the understanding of Christian worship.

ACKNOWLEDGMENTS

In addition to the above, many other resources have been particularly helpful in the preparation of this book, a few of which deserve special mention. *Words of Our Worship*, by Charles Mortimer Guilbert (New York: The Church Hymnal Corporation, 1988), and glossaries in numerous books put me on the trail of clear definitions. *A Survey of Christian Hymnody*, by William Jensen Reynolds (New York: Holt, Rinehart and Winston, 1963), was helpful in sketching a history of hymns. The many publications of the Monks of New Skete (Cambridge, N.Y. 12816) are invaluable resources of information and liturgy in the Eastern Orthodox tradition. *Corporate Worship in the Reformed Tradition*, by James Hastings Nichols (Philadelphia: Westminster Press, 1968), and *An Outline of Christian Worship*, by William D. Maxwell (New York: Oxford University Press, 1958), are persistent helps. Marion Hatchett's *Commentary on the American Prayer Book* (New York: Seabury Press, 1981), and *Manual on the Liturgy: Lutheran Book of Worship*, by Philip H. Pfatteicher and Carlos R. Messerli (Minneapolis: Augsburg Publishing House, 1979), contribute greatly to my appreciation of the Anglican and Lutheran traditions. Numerous books on Christian symbols are available, but particularly useful to me are *Seasons and Symbols: A Handbook on the Church Year*, by Robert Wetzler and Helen Huntington (Minneapolis: Augsburg Publishing House, 1962), and *Signs and Symbols in Christian Art*, by George Ferguson (New York: Oxford University Press, 1961). *Reformed Liturgy and Music*, a journal published by the Presbyterian Church (U.S.A.) and *Liturgy*, the journal of the Liturgical

Conference of Washington, D.C., are outstanding representatives of ecumenical liturgical thought, filled with pertinent and practical material.

There are many other resources I have consulted over a period of years, information that has become a part of my own liturgical understanding. There are especially those personal resources—teachers, professors, friends, and colleagues—who have informed and enlightened me over many years. I am grateful for their insights that have shaped my own.